SCORECARD

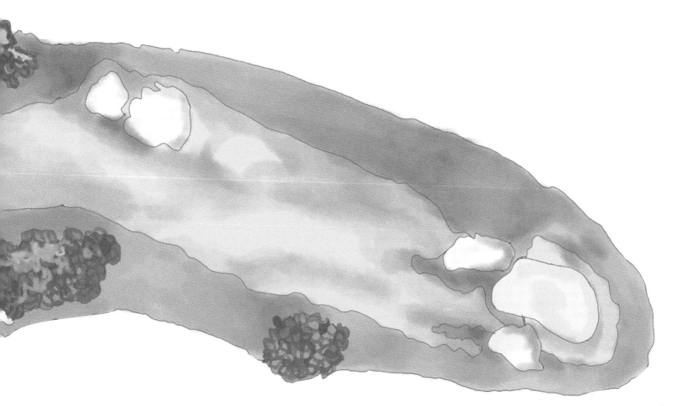

Sunday

10	11									400	405	3440	69	In	Tot
485	455														
4	4									4	4	36	72		
3	3	4	4	4	3	2	3	4						30	65

I HAVE CHECKED MY SCORE HOLE BY HOLE.

PLAYER SIGNATURE _____
Jack Nicklaus

THE 1986 MASTERS.

How Jack Nicklaus Roared Back to Win

John Boyette

with photography from

The Augusta Chronicle

LYONS PRESS
Guilford, Connecticut
An imprint of Globe Pequot Press

To my lovely wife, Kathy, who always believed in me.

To Mom, Dad, and Angela, the best parents and sister anyone could hope for.

To buy books in quantity for corporate use
or incentives, call **(800) 962–0973**
or e-mail **premiums@GlobePequot.com**.

Lyons Press is an imprint of Globe Pequot Press.

Photography © *Augusta Chronicle*

Text design: Sheryl Kober
Layout artist: Melissa Evarts
Project editor: Kristen Mellitt

Library of Congress Cataloging-in-Publication Data is available on file.

ISBN 978-0-7627-7758-7

Printed in the United States of America

10 9 8 7 6 5 4 3 2 1

An Interview with Jack Nicklaus 5

INTRODUCTION 9

CHAPTER 1   *Jones Cabin* 13

CHAPTER 2   *The Article* 17

CHAPTER 3   *The Putter* 27

CHAPTER 4   *Rise of Europe and the Global Golf Scene* 31

CHAPTER 5   *American Players* 45

CHAPTER 6   *Family Affair* 49

CHAPTER 7   *Down to Business* 55

CHAPTER 8   *Opening Day* .59

CHAPTER 9   *Making the Cut* 65

CHAPTER 10   *Moving Day* .73

CHAPTER 11   *The Front Nine* 81

CHAPTER 12   *The Final Nine Begins: No. 10* 87

CHAPTER 13   *Amen Corner* .91

CHAPTER 14   *Back on Track* 97

CHAPTER 15   *Hunting an Eagle* 103

CHAPTER 16   *Out of Hibernation* 107

CHAPTER 17   *Making Some Noise* 111

CHAPTER 18   *Coming Home* 117

Contents

CHAPTER 19   *The Remaining Challengers* 125

CHAPTER 20   *Sunday Night* 133

CHAPTER 21   *Media Coverage* 137

CHAPTER 22   *The Putter Part II* 143

CHAPTER 23   *Congratulations and Inspiration* 147

CHAPTER 24   *The Contenders* 149

CHAPTER 25   *Changes* 157

CHAPTER 26   *Saying Goodbye* 159

CHAPTER 27   *The Aftermath* 163

AFTERWORD   *Barbara Nicklaus Looks Back on 1986* 167

ACKNOWLEDGMENTS 171

PHOTOGRAPHY AND ILLUSTRATION CREDITS 173

INDEX 174

ABOUT THE AUTHOR 176

An Interview with Jack Nicklaus

Arriving at the Nicklaus Companies in North Palm Beach, Florida, for an appointment with Jack Nicklaus to talk about the 1986 Masters Tournament, I found myself walking through an inspiring gallery of mementos and tributes to the career of the game's greatest player.

With seventy-three PGA Tour wins and victories in eighteen professional majors and two U.S. Amateurs, Jack Nicklaus has plenty of triumphant moments on display. The 1986 Masters is well represented with photos of Nicklaus and his caddie and son Jackie from that week. A few depictions of Nicklaus sinking his famous putt on the 17th hole, with his oversized putter thrust into the air, also line the hallways leading to his private sanctuary.

But inside his corner office, there aren't any mementos from his playing days.

Instead, Nicklaus has personalized his space with family photos and keepsakes from his travels around the globe. Family is what has always driven Jack Nicklaus. And talk of family is what permeates our conversation about that memorable week.

Nicklaus is now seventy-one, and twenty-five years removed from what many consider his greatest triumph. He took time out from his busy schedule—he plays hardly any competitive golf, but his golf course design firm and other business pursuits keep him active—to sit down and recall how he shocked the sports world at the age of forty-six.

Coming into the 1986 Masters, Nicklaus was not among the favorites. He hadn't won anything in two years, and his last major title was a distant memory. He still enjoyed the competition, but it wasn't his primary focus.

"Golf was not a number one priority in my life, never was actually," Nicklaus says. "My family always was number one."

Jack Nicklaus, with a sterling replica of the Masters Trophy that is given to all winners by Augusta National Golf Club. Nicklaus is wearing a yellow shirt that commemorates his 1986 Masters victory.

And 1986 was all about family. His eldest son Jackie was his caddie, his mother and sister were in the gallery, and his wife and close friends surrounded Nicklaus as he roared back to win. The only person missing was Nicklaus's father, Charlie, who had passed away in 1970.

The two were extremely close, and Nicklaus interrupts the remembrance of '86 to tell a story of how they came to an understanding at the 1959 U.S. Amateur at The Broadmoor in Colorado Springs, Colorado.

"We were having dinner that night. And he said to me, 'That 14th hole, out there you hit this shot and don't you think it might have been better to . . .' I went [motions for a timeout]. I said 'Dad, you're my best friend, I love having you here, I want to have you here, but I've got to do this myself.'"

Nicklaus went on to win that U.S. Amateur with a 1-up victory over Charlie Coe in the 36-hole finale. It was the first major championship of his career, and the last time his father tried to give him advice on how to play golf.

"He was smart enough to know that," Nicklaus says.

The victory launched a career that saw Nicklaus win another U.S. Amateur, seventeen professional major championships, and seventy-two PGA Tour tournaments through the end of 1984. But he freely admits that by that point in his career, he was not putting the same effort into his game.

"Through the 60s and 70s, I used to start thinking about the Masters in January and start preparing in January to get ready for the Masters," he said. "Around the 80s, I started thinking about it in January and started preparing for it in the latter part of March. And that's sort of about where I was in '86."

That year, however, Nicklaus rolled back the clock to score perhaps the most unexpected, and most rewarding, victory of his career. Nicklaus played the final ten holes at Augusta National in 7-under par to beat some of the world's top players.

A lifetime of excellence in golf's biggest events had prepared Nicklaus to handle the emotions he felt that day.

"I've always felt like people have looked at me as calm and not very emotional when I played," he says. "Well, early in my career I got kind of emotional when I got into it and got excited, and I found I lost my concentration of playing. I tried very hard when I was younger to pull myself back and be able to be calm and be very controlled under the situations of pressure. And I think that's why I handled pressure well, because I learned to do that at a young age."

Nicklaus believes he was too caught up playing his game at the '86 Masters to realize the enormity of what he was achieving.

"No, I'm just a golfer playing a golf tournament, trying to do my best," he explains. "I hadn't won in two years, the last tournament I'd won was the Memorial Tournament in '84, and I didn't have any grandiose thoughts about let's win number eighteen type of thing. I found myself with an opportunity to win another golf tournament, and I sort of seized the moment and

I kept my composure, and I played well and I got some putts in and I won. After it's over, yeah, then you think about it."

The victory is still a fan favorite, Nicklaus says.

"I get so many people who come up to me and go, 'Oh Jack, I was in this restaurant and I stopped everything and watched television and never even finished my meal.' Or, 'I was in an airport and I was waiting on an airplane and I couldn't get on the airplane and I let the plane go.' People tell me all kinds of stories. Oh yeah, it's kind of neat. I still get them."

Not that Nicklaus dwelled on the accomplishment. He flew back home late that Sunday night and went back to his normal schedule the next day. "I probably came home and went to watch a golf match the next day or a baseball game," he says.

"Once I left the golf course the tournament was over. That's one of the reasons I'd say I went to the practice tee 98 percent of the time after I played. Not only to fix what I did wrong but to solidify what I did right. But also, you have a peace of mind, so when I went home at night I didn't have to carry golf with me. Maybe that's why I've been married fifty years."

Chalk it up to perfect timing.

An interest in golf. A love of the Masters Tournament and Augusta National Golf Club. A desire to see Jack Nicklaus. A budding journalism career. A promise kept.

All of those factors came together April 13, 1986 and put me in the middle of one of the most exciting days in the history of golf, or sports for that matter. Twenty-five years later, we're still talking and writing about it. I expect people will for as long as golf is played.

I grew up in Aiken, South Carolina, just a few miles across the Savannah River from Augusta and the Masters. I went to my first Masters in 1974, and I took up golf after my freshman year of high school in 1980. That summer, an aging Jack Nicklaus (he was 40) turned golf on its ear by winning the U.S. Open and PGA Championship. I was in awe of the Golden Bear.

I continued to attend the Masters, and in 1984 and 1985 I got to work on the leaderboard at the sixth hole thanks to being a member of the golf team at the University of South Carolina—Aiken. I had already expressed an interest in journalism, and by that time I was working part time for my hometown newspaper, the *Aiken Standard*.

In order to get a degree in journalism, though, I had to transfer to the main campus in Columbia. While at the University of South Carolina, I still worked for the paper and took any assignment thrown my way.

Bob Stoner had arrived as sports editor for the *Standard* about that time, and he was interested in doing things differently. Although the paper was known for its intense coverage of local events—it's called hyper-local now—Bob had an eye for bigger events. When he found that the *Standard* had traded the chance for two press credentials for four Masters badges, he immediately lobbied for a change to get credentials.

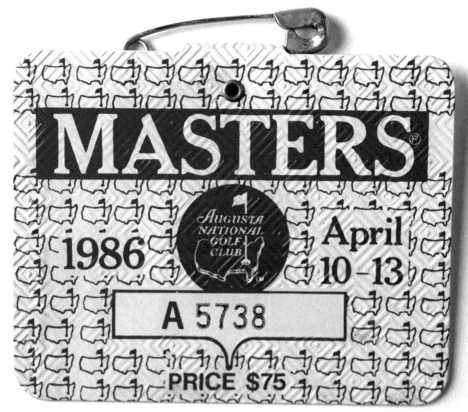

A Masters badge is one of the most coveted tickets in all of sports. The laminated plastic badges, particularly ones from the years that Jack Nicklaus won the Masters, are highly collectible.

Although he couldn't get the press credentials in 1986, Bob did have control of two patron badges. He promised I could use one of them on the weekend. I went on Saturday, and got there in time to see Nick Price finish off his course-record 63. Of course I focused on Nicklaus, and watched him shoot 69 and put himself in contention.

I was all geared up for Sunday's final round, but Bob's wife, Tammy, apparently had other plans. She wanted to go for the final round, and with no names on the badges, she could have easily taken my spot. But Bob held firm and said that he had promised it to me, and that was that.

I am forever in Bob's debt.

Once I arrived at the course, I decided to follow Nicklaus. I remember picking him up at the practice putting green and walking all eighteen holes with him. Some five hours and sixty-five shots later, it proved to be a wise decision.

It was a transcendent moment for everyone who witnessed it, and it spurred me on to a newspaper career where I could be close to the action and report on it firsthand. I spent the next nine years working at the *Aiken Standard,* and each spring I made the short pilgrimage to Augusta to cover the Masters.

In 1996 I took a position on the copy desk at the *Augusta Chronicle,* and for the next two Masters tournaments I worked on the daily wraparound sections that the *Chronicle* is well known for producing. It killed me to not be at the course, but I still felt I was a part of it as I edited stories and helped write headlines for the daily sections.

Sports editor Ward Clayton knew my background, and in 1998 he lobbied for me to be part of the reporting team that the *Chronicle* sent out to the course. That was another good year for Nicklaus as he was honored for forty years of competition, and he made a Sunday rally that gave him his best finish in years.

Two years later, Ward left to take a job with the PGA Tour. Thanks to my involvement with covering the tournament and my love for all things Masters, the editors chose me to take over as sports editor. Fourteen years after covering my first Masters, I had my dream job.

This book is the culmination of nearly twenty-five years' worth of conversations, memories, and interviews.

It's hanging around the big oak tree outside Augusta National's clubhouse and being able to talk to the great writers who also were there.

It's going on the road to interview golfers—most of them major championship winners—about their experiences in Augusta that week.

It's the opportunity to have been a part of numerous interview sessions with Jack Nicklaus through the years, and his recounting that memorable final round.

It's the chance to talk to Jackie about that afternoon and how nervous he was waiting in Jones Cabin.

It's reliving that special day nearly every day of my life, even if that means just looking at the framed magazine cover in my home office or the small photo of Nicklaus sinking his putt at the 17th that is tacked on the wall of my office cubicle.

Twenty-five years later, I hope you enjoy taking this journey back to the 1986 Masters as much as I enjoyed reliving that magical week for this book.

CHAPTER 1

Jones Cabin

Sunday, April 13, 1986

Jackie Nicklaus remembers the waiting.

After completing the final round of the 1986 Masters Tournament, Jack Nicklaus and his oldest son were whisked away to nearby Jones Cabin. It is Masters custom for the leader to stay in the Jones Cabin—located next to the 10th tee—if he finishes while golfers are still on the course. Eight golfers were still playing the Augusta National course, and half of them had a chance to catch Nicklaus, who had won the Masters a record five times.

"That's the first time I remember he couldn't sit still," said Jackie, who had served as caddie for his father for the first time in the Masters. "He was sitting on a couch, then walking back and forth. He couldn't control what was happening anymore."

For most golfers, waiting is the hardest part. Unlike a tennis player who stays on the court to fight his opponent until match point, a golfer who finishes his round first has little influence on the actions of his foes. All Nicklaus could do was sweat it out. Tom Kite, Seve Ballesteros, Greg Norman, and Nick Price all still had a chance to catch him after he putted out on the 18th hole to become the leader in the clubhouse.

Nicklaus had finished his round with a near-birdie on the final hole, and he embraced his son. Whatever happened now, Nicklaus had created an opportunity to add another chapter to his legendary career.

"I walked off the green knowing that I'd put myself in a position to win the golf tournament," Nicklaus said. "And Jackie was there—you know, everybody talks about the hug that Jackie and I had. I didn't think much about it because, you know, that's no different than I do with my son anytime. But I walked off and it's a great picture, I love the picture watching the two of us walk off."

Barbara Nicklaus joined her husband and son for the wait. "There was not a lot of conversation," she said.

Customs and traditions are everything at the Masters and Augusta National Golf Club, which was created by Bobby Jones and Clifford Roberts. Jones was the consummate amateur who retired at the peak of his powers; Roberts was the meticulous businessman who ruled the club and tournament with absolute authority.

Every action is planned in great detail, and no detail is small enough to go unnoticed.

That included the leader waiting in Jones Cabin. Golfers are usually accompanied by a tournament official, and they have a chance to watch the tournament unfold on television.

For Nicklaus, it was unusual territory. He was used to winning handily at the Masters, or at least being in the final group.

In 1963, he won a duel down the stretch by sinking a birdie putt on the 16th and became the youngest player to ever don a green jacket. In 1965, he overpowered the golf course and set records for total score and margin of victory that would last a generation. In 1966, he won a three-way playoff to become the tournament's first back-to-back champion. In 1972, he led after each round and was the only player under par for seventy-two holes.

In 1975, he played in the group in front of the final pairing of Tom Weiskopf and Johnny Miller. Nicklaus finished his round with a one-shot lead over those two, but had to wait a few nervous moments as Weiskopf and Miller knocked it close and had short birdie putts to forge a tie. Video highlights show Nicklaus peering out of the scoring building erected behind the 18th green. Both Weiskopf and Miller missed, and Nicklaus earned his fifth green jacket. That year there might not have been enough time for Nicklaus to be transported to the Jones Cabin, or perhaps he decided to wait it out and see the finish in person.

Exactly eleven years later to the day, though, he had no choice but to wait and reflect on a memorable week. Even for a Golden Bear—maybe especially for a player of Nicklaus's stature—the waiting was the hardest part.

Jack Nicklaus slips into his green jacket, with a helping hand from Gary Player, after winning the 1975 Masters. Nicklaus won a three-man shootout on the final day against Tom Weiskopf and Johnny Miller.

"[I] went in and sat down on the couch to watch what was happening. And as I sat down Norman started making birdies," Nicklaus said. "And so I got nervous, I got up and started walking around. And I said, well, they didn't make as many birdies when I walked around so I walked around the rest of the time. Not that I had much control over it."

CHAPTER 2

The Article

On April 6, 1986—one week before Jack Nicklaus would pace nervously in the Jones Cabin—Tom McCollister had published an article in the *Atlanta Journal-Constitution*. The piece was brutal in its honesty, a searing appraisal of Nicklaus's chances of adding a sixth green jacket.

"Nicklaus is gone, done. He just doesn't have the game anymore. It's rusted from lack of use. He's 46, and nobody that old wins the Masters."

McCollister had the courage to put in ink what many others privately thought. Nicklaus had done little to make anyone think he had a chance of winning a major again.

He was six years removed from his last major triumph, and five years from the last time he contended in Augusta. He had not won a PGA Tour event in two years, and his performance in 1986 left much to be desired. In seven events, he had earned just $4,403.75. His best showing was a tie for thirty-ninth at the Hawaiian Open.

Nicklaus was rarely skewered in the press. He enjoyed talking to the writers, and the writers in turn appreciated his candor.

"I've said this for years, and a lot of others appreciated it, he was the best interview room interview in all of sports," said Dave Anderson, columnist for the *New York Times*. "If you asked him a question, he gave you two or three paragraphs. A thoughtful answer, an explanatory answer. It didn't matter if it was me or [fellow writers] Dan Jenkins or Art Spander or someone from Dubuque, Iowa. If anyone still wanted him, he'd come off to the side and still answer questions. He'd do it as long as anyone wanted to."

Much has been made over McCollister's article, but in reality the Nicklaus portion was just one paragraph that consisted of those four sentences. His premise was that "the big names aren't playing well, and the new faces have no identifiable track records." McCollister lumped Nicklaus into a category of former winners, including Tom Watson, Ben Crenshaw, Raymond Floyd, and Craig Stadler. He wrote that "something's missing in each of them."

For Nicklaus, good health was missing in the three months leading up to the Masters.

In the *Augusta Chronicle*'s preview issue, Roger Whiddon pointed out that the Golden Bear had battled a flu bug as well as lingering pain in his elbow and back. "If I can ever get healthy again, I'll be just fine," Nicklaus said.

Whiddon wrote that Nicklaus had consulted with longtime mentor Jack Grout before the Masters to correct his "horrendous play this year."

"Basically, I took the hands out of my game," Nicklaus said in the article. "I was playing with too much hand, getting too violent in the hitting area."

Nicklaus also picked up a thing or two from his caddie son. Jackie was a fine golfer in his own right, but he had recently taken a short-game lesson from Chi Chi Rodriguez and he shared a tip with his father: Take the wrists out when chipping the ball as much as possible.

"He took me under his wing and showed me how to work the ball around the green," Jackie Nicklaus said. "He's an absolute magician."

No matter what Jack Nicklaus did at the 1986 Masters, his legacy was secure. He had more major championship victories—five Masters, five PGA Championships, four U.S. Opens, three British Opens, and two U.S. Amateurs—than anyone who had ever played the game. That included Augusta National and Masters co-founder Bobby Jones, a career amateur who amassed thirteen titles before retiring at 28 in 1930.

Plenty of other golfers tried to surpass Jones, but only Nicklaus was successful. That included pre–World War II greats like Harry Vardon and Walter Hagen, and stars of the 1940s and 1950s like Ben Hogan, Sam Snead, and Byron Nelson. Nicklaus beat contemporaries like Arnold Palmer, Gary Player, and Billy Casper more often than not. Of the current generation, only Tom Watson seemed to have Nicklaus's number. Of his eight major championships, four had come at Nicklaus's expense. That included the "Duel in the Sun" at the 1977 British Open at Turnberry, and the famous chip-in from the rough at Pebble Beach to win the U.S. Open in 1982. Nicklaus was runner-up in each of Watson's two Masters victories.

Nicklaus compiled a stellar amateur record, and he had success against the pros on the biggest stages. After missing the cut in his initial appearance at Augusta National in 1959, Nicklaus finished in the top fifteen the next three years.

He turned pro in 1962, and won his first major, the U.S. Open, that June. In a tense duel, Nicklaus defeated Arnold Palmer, golf's reigning king, in an eighteen-hole playoff at Oakmont Country Club, not far from where Palmer grew up.

That victory set the stage for a run of success that has rarely been seen in the game, and Augusta National and the Masters would figure prominently.

Nicklaus's first Masters win came in 1963. After a so-so 74 in the opening round, Nicklaus scorched Augusta National with a 6-under 66 that was the low round of the tournament. A 74 in the third round gave him a one-shot lead over Ed Furgol entering the final round.

Tony Lema, Sam Snead, and Julius Boros all made moves in the final round, and Nicklaus struggled. Through twelve holes, he was 2-over for the day. But a birdie at the 13th righted the ship, and when he got to the 16th hole he needed another one to ensure a victory. He knocked his tee shot to 12 feet of the cup, and he coaxed the delicate birdie putt into the hole.

Snead, a 50-year-old competing against players half his age, had pulled ahead with birdies at the 14th and 15th. But bogeys at 16 and 18 cost him a chance to win a fourth Masters.

Two airtight pars on the 17th and 18th gave Nicklaus a one-shot win over Lema, who had birdied the final hole to put pressure on Nicklaus. More importantly, the win made the 23-year-old Nicklaus the youngest Masters champion ever. He slipped into his green coat as others were sizing up his potential greatness.

"The size is 44 regular, and they may as well file it where it will be handy," Alfred Wright wrote in *Sports Illustrated*. "Jack may earn a few more of those coats in the future."

Nicklaus finished second to Palmer in 1964, but he was never really a contender. Palmer won by six strokes for what turned out to be his fourth, and final, Masters win. That seemed to restore some order to golf's universe, but Nicklaus crashed the party again at the 1965 Masters.

Nicklaus, Palmer, and Gary Player—golf's "Big Three"—were all tied for the lead after thirty-six holes. But what happened in the third round is the stuff of legend. Nicklaus made a slight adjustment in his putting stroke, and he promptly birdied five of the first eight holes. With three more on the second nine, Nicklaus's round of 64 matched the course record set by Lloyd Mangrum twenty-five years earlier.

The score put Nicklaus five clear of Player, who shot 69, and eight ahead of Palmer, who could do no better than 72. Nicklaus completed the tournament with 69, which gave him a total of 271 for seventy-two holes. That shattered the previous record of 274 set by Ben Hogan, and his nine-stroke margin of victory over Palmer and Player also broke the existing mark.

No less of an authority than Bobby Jones said it was the greatest tournament performance he had ever seen. "Nicklaus played a game with which I am not familiar," Jones said.

In four seasons as a pro, Nicklaus had set the record as youngest Masters winner and held or shared every major scoring record at Augusta National (round, seventy-two-hole total, and margin of victory). He was halfway to matching Palmer's record of four Masters titles.

No one had won at Augusta National in consecutive years, but Nicklaus changed that in 1966. He needed an eighteen-hole playoff to do it, and his round of 70 defeated Tommy Jacobs by two and Gay Brewer by eight.

The victory, though, gave Nicklaus a dilemma. Custom called for the defending champion to help the new winner into his green coat. Bobby Jones spoke up at the closing ceremony.

"Cliff [Roberts] and I have discussed the problem, and have decided you will just have to put the coat on yourself," Jones said. That wasn't a problem for Nicklaus.

Even if he was the perennial favorite, Nicklaus didn't win the Masters every year. His stranglehold on the tournament slipped from 1967 to 1971, as it was a time of transformation for Nicklaus. The late 1960s were a time of social and political upheaval, and Nicklaus was not immune to change. Once derisively called Fat Jack because of his weight, Nicklaus slimmed down and treated himself to a new wardrobe and wore his hair longer. He morphed into the Golden Bear, and his new ventures included trying his hand at golf course design and other business pursuits.

Nicklaus regained his touch at the Masters in 1972. He led all the way from his opening 68 and, strangely enough, his scores were progressively higher. He followed with rounds of 71, 73, and 74, but he still won by three shots over Bruce Crampton, Bobby Mitchell, and Tom Weiskopf. He matched Palmer's record of four Masters wins.

Nicklaus was closing in on Jones's record of thirteen majors, but he also was in pursuit of another Jones feat: the Grand Slam. If he could win all four of golf's majors in a single year, he would match a similar feat set by Jones in 1930 when he won the British Amateur, British Open, U.S. Open, and U.S. Amateur.

After winning the second leg at the U.S. Open at Pebble Beach, Nicklaus's run ended when he lost the British Open at Muirfield by one shot to Lee Trevino.

Nicklaus usually won his majors in unspectacular fashion. He would play his game, protect par, and let others make mistakes. He had rarely been involved in a good old-fashioned shootout.

That changed in 1975. He opened with rounds of 68 and 67, and his fifth Masters win looked like a formality. But he opened the door with a 73 in the third round, and Tom Weiskopf charged ahead with 66. Johnny Miller, one of the streakiest players in the game's history, shot 65 and was only three back.

The final round was epic as the three men jockeyed for position. Nicklaus wound up trailing Weiskopf and Miller, but he pulled closer when he two-putted the 15th for birdie. Weiskopf also birdied the 15th, and the gallery's roar told Nicklaus what he must do. "That is evil music ringing in Nicklaus's ears," CBS announcer Ben Wright said.

On the par-3 16th, Nicklaus delivered the crushing blow: a 40-footer that sent him running around the green in celebration. When Nicklaus's unlikely putt fell, CBS announcer Henry Longhurst was quick with a response. "That has to be the greatest putt I ever saw in my life. And now Weiskopf will have to take it as he dished it out before."

Both Weiskopf and Miller had short birdie chances to tie Nicklaus at the 18th, but both missed. Nicklaus, for the fifth time, was a Masters winner.

Jack Nicklaus watches a putt during the final round of the 1975 Masters. Nicklaus shot a final-round 68, highlighted by a 40-foot birdie on the 16th, to win his fifth Masters.

"In all the time I have played golf, I thought this was the most exciting display I had ever seen," Nicklaus said at the time.

The victory was Nicklaus's 13th major title as a professional, and he added another four months later when he won the PGA Championship. Counting his two U.S. Amateur victories, Nicklaus had surpassed his idol Jones's record with room to spare.

Nicklaus won the 1978 British Open at St. Andrews, and at 38 years old most figured he was done winning majors. It would be a nice way for him to go out, on a course he loved so much. And Nicklaus played like he was done in 1979, the first year since he turned pro that he was winless. The critics began circling him as the 1980 season approached, but the 40-year-old Nicklaus wasn't done yet.

After a mediocre showing at the Masters, a tie for 33rd that was his worst finish since missing the cut in 1967, Nicklaus rolled back the clock at the U.S. Open. He opened with a 63 at Baltusrol, matching the lowest score ever shot in a major, and won a memorable duel with Isao Aoki for his fourth U.S. Open title. Two months later, Nicklaus put on a clinic at Oak Hill to win the PGA Championship by seven strokes.

Nicklaus now says he isn't sure why he kept playing after 1980. He was still ten years away from being eligible for the Senior Tour, but that wasn't a big motivation.

"My business didn't take full time, I still enjoyed playing golf, [but] I didn't really work very hard," Nicklaus said. "It was keeping my hand in the game, enjoying playing golf, enjoying being part of what was going on. Was I grinding to try to create a better record? Not particularly. Could I have or should I have? Maybe so. Would I have had better results? Yeah, probably. But I really wasn't motivated to do a whole lot. When 1986 rolled around I didn't have a big motivation."

Always a devoted father, Nicklaus took even more time to spend with his five children.

"I didn't want to go out and play golf tournaments when my kids were involved with events at school," he said. "I spent more time with them and doing things they were doing than things I was doing."

Coming into 1986, Nicklaus had not won a major since Oak Hill—a span of five years and twenty majors. But he had contended a few times in those five years, and he had won two PGA Tour events. Nicklaus, though, said his expectations were still lofty.

"I still expect to play well, I expect to play like I did ten, fifteen years ago," Nicklaus told the *Chronicle*. "But I'm not the Jack of age 25 and 35. I'm 46 years old. I still want to win and think I can. If nothing else, I'm gonna do it just to show you guys I still can."

Even if Nicklaus thought he could win, others didn't. That included *Golf Digest*, where Nicklaus was chief playing editor. Each year in its April issue, the magazine listed an early form chart for Masters contenders. But that year Nicklaus was nowhere to be found. Seve Ballesteros was the 8–1 favorite, followed by Watson at 10–1. Previous winners Floyd, Langer, and Fuzzy Zoeller were listed, as were longshots Scott Verplank and Corey Pavin.

McCollister's article picked several possible winners, including Ballesteros, Fred Couples, and Tom Kite. Of Ballesteros, he wrote that the Spaniard had been spurned by the PGA Tour and "might just want to make his point, and there's no better place to do it." On Couples, he gushed that he was "long and strong where needed and short and sweet when he has to be." For Kite, McCollister opined that he "might be your winner. He's due after eight top-six finishes in the past ten years."

Nicklaus didn't see McCollister's article on the day it was published, but it would soon become a focal point.

At a rented house in the suburbs of Augusta, friends of Nicklaus who were staying with him that week began to arrive. That included John Montgomery and his wife, Nancy, who made the annual trip.

Nicklaus and Montgomery's relationship went back to the old Jacksonville Open. A former football player at Duke, Montgomery served in the Army and worked for the FBI before landing a position with Southern Bell that eventually took him to Jacksonville, Florida. Montgomery later formed his own golf management company, Executive Sports. When Nicklaus began his Memorial Tournament in 1976, Montgomery helped it become one of the best-run events on the PGA Tour.

Nicklaus and Montgomery enjoyed playing practical jokes on each other, and Montgomery decided to have some fun with Nicklaus that week. Montgomery's son lived in Atlanta and had seen the article. He got it to his father, who taped the article in a place Nicklaus was sure to see it: the refrigerator.

"He is known for putting chickens in my yard, goats in my yard, donkeys in my yard, horse manure in my yard, tacking outhouses and bears onto my trees and so forth and so on," Nicklaus said. "One more little article that he thought was cute to put on the refrigerator was nothing more for Montgomery."

Montgomery denied having anything to do with it, Barbara Nicklaus said. "He knew he'd put it in the perfect place," she said. "Jack didn't take it down, didn't say anything, never mentioned it to John."

Nicklaus said he laughed when he first saw the article, but admitted the words were irritating.

"Did it motivate me? It might have. I can't imagine an article motivating me," he said. "It was fun, it was a good joke, having fun with it. The article could have been there the year before, two years before that, anytime before that, it just happened to fall on that year."

CHAPTER 3

The Putter

The forerunner of MacGregor Golf began in Dayton, Ohio, in 1897. Company founder Edward Canby wanted to mass produce golf clubs and get in on the golf boom that swept the nation in the early part of the twentieth century.

With the transition from hickory to steel shafts, MacGregor made a name for itself with numerous innovations and adopted the slogan "the greatest name in golf." Ben Hogan, Byron Nelson, and Jimmy Demaret—all Masters champions—were among the pros who played MacGregor.

The company continued to flourish, and by the 1950s MacGregor boasted that more than half of the touring pros used its equipment. The company might have made its wisest move in 1961 when it signed a young professional named Jack Nicklaus for a reported $100,000. The two would be linked for more than two decades and MacGregor would be a part of all of Nicklaus's major championship wins. In the late 1970s, Nicklaus and a MacGregor executive took control of the company, which had moved its operations to Albany, Georgia.

Fast-forward to the mid-1980s, when Clay Long was MacGregor's chief of research and development. He had been charged by Nicklaus to come up with a putter that resembled the Ping Pal model being used by Tom Watson, who used the blade-style putter to supplant Nicklaus as the top American player and win several majors.

What Long and his fellow workers came up with was a putter with a corrective face that had an overhang. But in order to make it functional for those who used a forward press—the overhang would hit the ball before the face—Long decided to make a version that was scaled up 32 percent.

That made the overall putter super-sized, and he made a half dozen to test out. "We had tested it and several of us used it and it was solid and rolled the ball very well," Long said.

But the U.S. Golf Association said it didn't conform to its standards and couldn't be used in competition. So Long made one without the overhang, and it became a putter with a huge moment of inertia. Or, in other words, it wasn't prone to twisting or turning when the putter face struck the golf ball.

"We said, 'What if we're going to sell this as the most forgiving putter out there?'" Long said. "But it was such a goofy looking thing."

Nicklaus had yet to see the new putter, but he did when he came to a sales meeting in Albany in June 1985. "He came over to my office, and we had Astroturf carpet in our lab," Long said. "I pulled one out and said look at this. He said, 'Is this a joke?' I said no, hit a couple putts with it."

After hitting a couple of test putts, Nicklaus agreed to try the putter out. "I sent some down to Palm Beach and about two weeks later I got a call from him," Long said. "He said that putter's not too bad. It rolls the ball good."

Long asked Nicklaus if he thought it had potential as a product in the MacGregor line. "And Jack said yes," Long said.

The Response ZT—the ZT stood for zero twist—was born.

Long relayed his conversations with Nicklaus to company president George Nichols, and MacGregor decided to produce four models and introduce them in 1986. With production in full swing, Nicklaus continued to use the oversized putter. At the Loxahatchee Club in Jupiter, Florida, Nicklaus shot a course record using the putter. "We get word that he's played really well with this goofy putter," Long said.

At the annual PGA merchandise show in Orlando, Florida, in January 1986, Long and his team distributed five hundred putters. Nicklaus, meanwhile, had put the "MI 615" version in his bag for the start of the season. His model was the only one painted black.

MacGregor had forecast that it would sell six thousand of the putters that year, but by the time of the Masters the company had already sold twenty thousand of the putters that retailed for $62 each.

But with golfers being notoriously fickle with their equipment and especially their putters, there was no guarantee Nicklaus would keep using it. "We were scared to death he would quit using it because he was playing so poorly," Long said.

The first time Nicklaus used the putter in competition was at the Honda Classic, about a month before the Masters. On a very windy day, Nicklaus almost gave up on the putter after a gaffe.

"I remember it was so light that I had about a four-inch putt and the wind blew the putter into the ball and moved it two inches," he said. "I was ready to can that putter."

Nicklaus missed the cut that week, but decided to stick with the putter. In interviews before the Masters, he acknowledged that the new putter had alleviated his problems on the greens that had plagued him the last two years.

"My play earlier this year was horrendous," Nicklaus said. "My putting has been the only consistent part. I've changed putters and I'm using a Mac-Gregor with a big head."

Leading up to the Masters, Nicklaus always visited Augusta National for practice rounds. Since he couldn't play without being accompanied by a member, he would usually play with William S. Morris III, publisher of the *Augusta Chronicle* and chairman and chief executive officer of Morris Communications Co. The two had become friends over the years, and in 1986 Nicklaus paid his usual visit.

Morris said Nicklaus was playing well and sinking everything with his new putter. "We were on the 14th hole and I said, 'Jack, let me putt with that.' He said sure, and I putted one right in the hole," Morris said.

"He said, 'You like that putter?' I said I sure did," Morris replied.

"'Keep it,' he said. 'You can have it, it's yours.'"

Morris didn't want to take something away from Nicklaus that he used in competition, but the golfer insisted.

"No, I've got another one in the bag," Nicklaus told him. "They sent me two."

CHAPTER 4

Rise of Europe and the Global Golf Scene

The American public might have been surprised by the rise of Europe in golf's biggest events, but those close to the game could see it coming.

The revolution began in 1979, when continental European players were first eligible to join their Great Britain and Ireland counterparts on the Ryder Cup team, and a young Spaniard named Severiano Ballesteros was emerging on the scene.

Ballesteros had contended at the British Open as a teen, and he broke through in 1979 with a victory at Royal Lytham & St. Annes. His movie-star good looks, boyish charm, and swashbuckling style of play made him a fan favorite.

In 1980, Ballesteros overwhelmed Augusta National and won the Masters in a romp. The 23-year-old threatened to break the seventy-two-hole scoring record, but a few errant shots on the final nine holes made the final margin closer than it really was. He broke Jack Nicklaus's record as the youngest Masters champion, and experts predicted that he would have a good chance of breaking Nicklaus's other records at Augusta.

In 1983, Ballesteros added a second Masters title to his resume. With weather forcing a Monday finish, Ballesteros started the final round with two birdies and an eagle in his first four holes. He strolled to a four-shot win over Ben Crenshaw and Tom Kite.

Europe was starving for a golf hero. Until Ballesteros, no European had won a major championship since Tony Jacklin's triumph at the 1970 U.S. Open. Europe had produced several worthy players, but none could crack an American lineup that included the likes of Nicklaus, Miller, Weiskopf, Trevino, and Watson. Throw in South African Gary Player, and the deck was stacked against the Europeans.

(Above left) Seve Ballesteros looks on after putting during the 1980 Masters. (Above right) Ballesteros blasts out of a bunker. (Left) Ballesteros acknowledges the gallery as he strolls to a four-shot victory. Ballesteros became the first European player to win at Augusta National and just the second international player to win the Masters. He would win more than seventy professional tournaments during his career, including five majors. He was inducted into the World Golf Hall of Fame in 1999.

Hope was on the horizon, and not just from Ballesteros. Englishman Nick Faldo was on the verge of breaking through, and a young German who had suffered from the yips also was becoming a contender.

Bernhard Langer was very familiar with Ballesteros, and he looked to the young Spaniard as a role model. "He was the next guy who won the Masters and the British Open, and he was proof that (a European) can become a world beater," Langer said.

In 1985, Langer won seven times on five continents. That included his back-to-back wins at the Masters and the Heritage on Hilton Head Island, South Carolina.

The Europeans hadn't beaten the Americans in the Ryder Cup since 1957, but with the addition of Ballesteros their odds improved. In 1983, the U.S. team that was captained by Nicklaus held on to win by one point thanks to a clutch shot by Lanny Wadkins on the final hole.

By 1985, though, the advantage had shifted to Europe. Langer won the Masters in a duel with Ballesteros to become just the third foreign-born player to win in Augusta. At the British Open that summer, Scotland's Sandy Lyle gave the home crowd something to cheer about with his victory.

Bernhard Langer gestures at his ball after missing a putt during the 1985 Masters. Langer overcame putting woes, including a bout with the yips, to become a major champion.

"There was a large group of guys that came through at the same time and they were very competitive and they pushed each other," American Tom Kite said. "It made Europe a definite force."

At the Ryder Cup Matches at The Belfry that fall, the Europeans didn't let up. With Ballesteros winning three of his four matches in the two days of foursomes and four-ball play, the Europeans held a 9–7 lead over Lee Trevino's American squad. Nicklaus had been a staple of American teams for years, but he wasn't part of the team in 1985.

The American team featured Masters champions Raymond Floyd, Fuzzy Zoeller, and Craig Stadler, along with major champions like Wadkins, Hubert Green, and Andy North. With that mix of veterans and solid performers like Kite and Curtis Strange, most felt the Americans could rally in the twelve Sunday singles matches and retain the trophy.

It didn't happen. Only Stadler, Strange, and Green could win their singles matches, and Kite halved his battle with Ballesteros. Europe took 7½ points the final day for a decisive 16½ to 11½ victory over the Americans. When Sam Torrance clinched the Ryder Cup with a birdie putt on the 18th hole, the victory sent shock waves across the Atlantic.

Even if the Americans were down, they figured to recapture the Ryder Cup when the matches were held in 1987. It would be on familiar ground— Jack Nicklaus would be the captain, and his Muirfield Village course in Ohio would be the venue—and the Americans had never lost the matches on home soil.

Even though Europe was on top of the golf world, only three members of the victorious Ryder Cup team made it to Augusta in 1986: Ballesteros, Langer, and Lyle. The other nine members—Manuel Pinero, Ian Woosnam, Paul Way, Sam Torrance, Howard Clark, Jose Rivero, Nick Faldo, Jose Maria Canizares, and Ken Brown—fell victim to a change in qualifications announced by the Masters in November 1985.

Augusta National had traditionally invited members of the most recent European Ryder Cup team to play, but that changed for 1986. Club and tournament chairman Hord Hardin explained that it was because of the size of the field.

"We were up to the high 70s at that point of people who had already qualified," Hardin said. "The trend was already obvious there were going to be more names winning some of those (PGA Tour) tournaments who were going to become eligible who were not otherwise eligible."

1986 MASTERS TOURNAMENT QUALIFICATIONS

1. Masters Champions (Lifetime Invitation)

2. U.S. Open Champions (Honorary, non-competing after 5 years)

3. U.S. Amateur Champions (Honorary, non-competing after 2 years)

4. British Open Champions (Honorary, non-competing after 5 years)

5. British Amateur Champions (Honorary, non-competing after 2 years)

6. PGA Champions (Honorary, non-competing after 5 years)

7. U.S. Ryder Cup Team

8. U.S. Walker Cup Team

9. First 24 players, including ties, in the previous Masters Tournament

10. First 16 players, including ties, in U.S. Open Championship

11. First 8 players, including ties, in the PGA Championship

12. Semi-finalists in U.S. Amateur Championship

13. Top 30 leaders from the PGA Tour Official Money List for the previous calendar year

14. PGA Co-sponsored Tour Tournament winners (classified by the Tournament Players Division as one of its major events) from finish of the last Masters to start of the next Masters

Source: Augusta National Golf Club

Another factor, Hardin said, was the weak individual performances of several of the European Ryder Cuppers. Outside of Ballesteros, Langer, and Lyle, Hardin said Clive Clark's victory in the World Cup might have put him closest to eligibility.

"But, every one of you knows that the World Cup field is not the same as the British Open or the U.S. Open and many U.S. tournaments," Hardin said.

The American Ryder Cup team still received automatic invitations, but most of those players were already eligible. Only Andy North, who withdrew because of an injury to his right hand, failed to show up in Augusta in 1986.

Only four Europeans were in the field of eighty-eight players for the 1986 Masters. Ballesteros and Langer were in as past champions, and Lyle had qualified as British Open champion. Northern Ireland's Garth McGimpsey, the British Amateur winner, rounded out the quartet.

The field contained only fifteen foreigners, including the four Europeans. What Europe lacked in quantity it more than made up for in quality with the world's top two players, according to the Sony Ranking, in Ballesteros and Langer. Those former champions were favored at Augusta.

Sandy Lyle, however, was not getting much attention leading up to Augusta. But that changed overnight with his victory at the Greater Greensboro Open the week before the Masters. The Scot's two-shot victory over Andy Bean was his first on American soil, and he said it took a "large monkey" off his back. As golfers and members of the press began to trickle into Augusta on Monday, April 7, the focus turned to the soft-spoken Lyle. Even though he was worn out, Lyle decided to get in a trip around Augusta National.

Lyle had a dozen European Tour victories to his credit, but he had not challenged in four previous Masters trips. His highlight had come in the second round in 1985, when he shot 7-under 65. But he followed it up with rounds of 76 and 73 and wound up tied for 25th, his best showing in the major.

The long-hitting Lyle received a boost with his afternoon practice round. "The way I'm driving, it should make the course a lot easier," he told the *Augusta Chronicle*. "I can gain a lot of yardage off my tee shots. It will be an advantage. Like at 13, I can get around the corner, and use a 5-iron to the green."

Lyle wasn't getting much buzz before his win in Greensboro, but the win stamped him as a player to watch. He didn't put his first PGA Tour win on the same level as taking the Claret Jug at Royal St. George's, but he did stress its importance.

"Both of them meant a lot to me. The British Open is a big major, in my mind," he said. "Greensboro is not as much of a major, I suppose, as the British Open. But it means a lot. It was my first in America."

Sandy Lyle was Jack Nicklaus's playing partner in the final round of the 1986 Masters. Two years later, Lyle would win the Masters with a birdie on the final hole.

While Lyle was celebrating his first win on U.S. soil, Ballesteros was settling in for a long skirmish with the PGA Tour. The Spaniard and PGA Tour commissioner Deane Beman were having a nasty public feud over the number of events players were required to participate in to retain their membership.

Ballesteros, who spent most of his time on the European Tour, only played in nine events on the PGA Tour in 1985. That was short of the required fifteen, and Beman suspended Ballesteros's membership for 1986.

As a former champion Ballesteros could play at the Masters as long as he wished. The PGA Tour didn't run the tournament. The Spaniard pointed out that he played a full schedule in Europe, and that meeting the minimum requirement for the PGA Tour would be too demanding. Beman, though, refused to relent.

"Beman is a little man who wants to be big," Ballesteros said at the Masters. "Let's forget about him."

The bottom line for Ballesteros was that he came to Augusta with only two and a half tournaments under his belt leading up to the Masters. He played in an event in Spain, and a satellite event in Florida. His most recent event came at the USF&G Classic in New Orleans, where he was the defending champion. But he missed the cut.

Ballesteros joked that the most money he had won all year had come in a practice round Sunday at Augusta National. But he dismissed the notion that his game was rusty. "I've been hitting balls and practicing; that's OK," he said.

While Europeans were getting the lion's share of attention, golfers from Australia, Japan, and South Africa also expected to be a factor at the Masters.

Aussie Greg Norman, known as the "Great White Shark" for his exploits down under, was chief among those. He had made quite a splash in his Masters debut in 1981, finishing alone in fourth. With booming tee shots and a deft touch on the greens, after that initial performance most figured he would be an annual contender.

He had won twice on the PGA Tour in 1984, and his victories around the world were starting to pile up. But for some reason he had not done much at Augusta National. He had made the cut each year from 1982 to 1985, but his best finish was a tie for twenty-fifth in 1984.

Two players from Japan, Tsuneyuki (Tommy) Nakajima and Isao Aoki, were ranked in the top twenty of the initial Sony Rankings. Nakajima was ranked seventh, but he was better known for a pair of dubious achievements on some of golf's biggest stages.

Tommy Nakajima studies a putt during the 1986 Masters. The Japanese golfer matched or broke par in all four rounds and tied for eighth.

At the 1978 Masters, Nakajima took a 13 on the par-5 13th hole to set a record for highest score on a single hole in tournament history. (Tom Weiskopf matched it with a 13 on the par-3 12th in 1980.) Nakajima's misery included several misadventures with the tributary of Rae's Creek that guards the hole. That included a two-shot penalty when he tried to play out of the water and his ball bounced off his shoe, and another two-shot penalty when he tried to hand his club to his caddie but the sand wedge touched the water. An interpreter who handled the exchange between Nakajima and reporters said the golfer "lost count."

Three months later, Nakajima shared the lead at the British Open at St. Andrews late in the third round. But on the infamous Road Hole, Nakajima putted his ball off the putting surface into the tricky greenside bunker, and took four shots to get out. His 9 knocked him out of contention and the British press quickly dubbed the event "the sands of Nakajima."

Aoki, meanwhile, was an infrequent Masters competitor who was best known in the United States for pushing Jack Nicklaus to the brink in the 1980 U.S. Open. Aoki played with Nicklaus all four rounds at Baltusrol, and he even broke the existing seventy-two-hole scoring record, but lost to the 40-year-old Nicklaus. His best showing at the Masters was sixteenth in 1985.

South Africa's Gary Player was the dean of international players—he was the first foreign-born Masters winner—and he also set the record as oldest winner when he made his stirring comeback in the final round of 1978.

Player won his first green jacket in 1961 when defending champion Arnold Palmer took a double bogey 6 on the final hole. Palmer and amateur Charlie Coe finished one shot behind the diminutive South African.

Player promptly challenged Augusta National chairman Clifford Roberts by keeping the new garment in South Africa. When he took it home following a playoff loss to Palmer in 1962, Roberts called to find out where it was. Custom called for the jackets to stay on club property at all times, except for the winner's one-year grace period.

According to Player, here's how the exchange went:

"'Gary, have you got the jacket?'

"I said, 'Yes, I do.'"

"He said, 'Well, no one ever takes the jacket away from here.'"

"And I said, 'Well, Mr. Roberts, if you want it, why don't you come and fetch it?'"

Roberts, who didn't lose many arguments, agreed to a compromise. "He kind of chuckled and said don't wear it in public," Player said.

Gary Player watches a shot during the 1986 Masters. Player, the first international champion at the Masters, had won at Augusta National three times.

Player would go another thirteen years before winning his second green jacket, in 1974. A brilliant 9-iron approach on the 17th hole in the final round set up an easy birdie for Player, who won by two shots over Dave Stockton and Tom Weiskopf.

Player saved his best win for his most improbable at Augusta. In 1978, Player was 42 years old and didn't figure to be a factor. But he carded seven birdies in the final ten holes, shot 64, and shocked the field to become the tournament's oldest winner.

But that was 1978, not 1986, and no one was seriously considering the 50-year-old Player to win a fourth green jacket.

NEW RANKINGS SYSTEM

Mark McCormack never won a major championship or served as a leader for one of golf's governing bodies. But his influence has lasted more than half a century and earned him a spot in the World Golf Hall of Fame.

McCormack was the agent who signed Arnold Palmer. Gary Player and Jack Nicklaus soon followed, and the "Big Three" were a marketing dream. McCormack tapped into their excellence on the course to create lucrative endorsement opportunities off it, most notably with Palmer, and his International Management Group became the premier sports agency in the world.

McCormack had published an unofficial ranking of golfers in his *World of Professional Golf Annual* from 1968 to 1985. Golf had always used victories and money lists as its unofficial ranking systems, but McCormack yearned for something more. The week before the 1986 Masters, he unveiled a new index that ranked players on their performances week in and week out.

The first issue of the Sony Ranking debuted April 6, 1986. It was the forerunner of the Official World Golf Ranking, the current system.

At the top was Bernhard Langer, followed by Seve Ballesteros in second. Scotland's Sandy Lyle and Americans Tom Watson and Mark O'Meara rounded out the top five. Greg Norman was sixth, followed by Japan's Tommy Nakajima, Hal Sutton, Corey Pavin, and Calvin Peete.

The ranking system reflected golf's global reach with six different countries represented in the top ten. The system gave points (and subtracted them) for performances in 1983, 1984, and 1985, with weighting toward the most recent years. For 1986, the first fourteen weeks of the season were evaluated.

Langer had 1,056 points to Ballesteros's 1,002. They were the only two players above 1,000 points. Langer cited Ballesteros as his inspiration, even if his memory is faulty about who was the first No. 1. "I was beating him about as often as he was beating me. He was world No. 1, and I shouldn't be too far behind him if I played well," Langer said. "So it was an encouragement to all of us—if he could do it, we could do it too."

Not everyone was in favor of the new ranking system.

"I was very much against it, to tell you the truth," said Norman, an Australian who was winless on the PGA Tour in 1985 and early in 1986. "It was very much top-heavy for top performances and didn't take away for bad performances, and it's still that way. Consistency good or bad should be taken into consideration."

(Left) Bernhard Langer acknowledges the patrons during the final round of the 1985 Masters. The victory was one of seven worldwide victories for Langer, who was listed as No. 1 when the Sony Ranking debuted in April 1986. (Below) Ben Crenshaw (left) helps Bernhard Langer into his green jacket in 1985. Langer held off playing partner Seve Ballesteros, as well as Raymond Floyd and Curtis Strange, with a final-round 68.

A bevy of young American stars were prominent on the second ten, but you had to go all the way down to No. 33 to find Jack Nicklaus's name on the Sony Ranking. Not surprisingly, he had not earned any points for his play in 1986. In fact, sixty-five points had been subtracted from his total.

"Where was I on that list?" Nicklaus asked. "Hundred something?" [Told he was 33rd.] "I was that high? In '86? They've refined it since then."

Today, the Official World Golf Ranking is endorsed by all six major professional men's tours and the organizations that conduct the four major championships. Points are accumulated over two years, and emphasis is placed on recent performances. The Masters now uses the world ranking to help determine its field, as do other events.

In recent years, more than half of the Masters field has been made up of foreign-born golfers. If the Official World Golf Ranking criteria had been in place in 1986, a few more Europeans would have made the trip to Augusta.

From its inception through the end of 2010, a total of thirteen golfers had held the No. 1 ranking with Tiger Woods spending the most time at the top with 623 weeks.

CHAPTER 5

American Players

In 1986 Arnold Palmer and Jack Nicklaus were the biggest names in American golf, even if Palmer was 56 and Nicklaus was 46.

Palmer had long ruled the Masters, and Arnie's Army was famous for following its general through the valleys and hills of Augusta National. A Palmer charge always brought some of the loudest roars.

The four-time champion had last been a serious threat at the Masters nearly twenty years before, but he wouldn't miss a trip to Augusta for anything. The two were practically synonymous, with Palmer arriving on the scene at about the same time television was gaining popularity. With his charisma and go-for-broke style, Palmer and the small screen were a perfect match.

"The camera either loves you or hates you. The camera fell in love with him, standing there next to his caddie, hitching his trousers, wrinkling his nose, flipping a cigarette to the ground. He hitched his trousers again and grabbed a club from his caddie. And he hits it on the green," said longtime CBS producer Frank Chirkinian, who recalled the first time he saw Palmer at the Masters in 1959.

"I thought, 'Holy mackerel, who is this guy?' He absolutely fired up the screen. It was quite obvious this was the star. We followed him all the way."

Palmer's first Masters win, in 1958, featured a rules controversy over a free drop at the 12th hole. Palmer got the ruling to go in his favor, and he won by a stroke. Two years later, Palmer revealed a flair for the dramatic by making birdies on the final two holes to edge a helpless Ken Venturi by one shot. In 1962, Palmer won the tournament's first three-way playoff with a brilliant 68. Two years later, in what would be his final hurrah in a major, Palmer overpowered Nicklaus and the rest of the field for a six-stroke win.

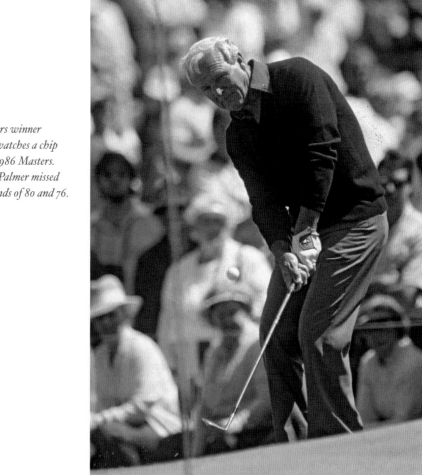

Four-time Masters winner Arnold Palmer watches a chip shot during the 1986 Masters. The 56-year-old Palmer missed the cut with rounds of 80 and 76.

Palmer's last PGA Tour win came in 1973, but he approached every year with the hope that he would recapture the old magic and win one final time. Even if he couldn't beat the younger players, Palmer could still hold his own on the relatively new Senior Tour.

A few weeks before the 1986 Masters, Palmer taped a television interview and explained why he was still playing. He also took a playful jab at Nicklaus, who had always said he would never become a ceremonial golfer.

"I'm going to be there trying to win. I remember when Jack said, about fifteen years ago, he said to me, 'Well, I tell you what, I will never be playing golf out here when I'm 35–40, I will be through.' I said, 'Well, Jack, you can come watch me, because I'm still going to be playing,'" Palmer said with a smile.

"And I read an article the other day where Jack, at 46, and still playing, said he felt like a man at 46 ought to be able to win a golf tournament. And I don't disagree with him, matter of fact I think he's right, he can still win a golf tournament. And if you can win at 46, I'm not sure you can't win at 56. You just have to get it all together at one time."

Whether either Palmer or Nicklaus could get it together one more time at Augusta remained to be seen. More puzzling was the play of 36-year-old Tom Watson, the top-ranked American in the field.

Like Nicklaus, Watson was in a bit of a slump coming into the 1986 Masters. He had not won on the PGA Tour since 1984, and he was three years removed from his fifth British Open win.

Still, the two-time Masters winner couldn't be counted out. Since holding off Nicklaus in 1981 at Augusta National, he had posted four consecutive top-ten finishes.

Tom Watson watches a putt on the 10th green in the final round of the 1986 Masters. Watson, who had won four of his majors at the expense of Jack Nicklaus, could do no better than a 71 and a tie for sixth this time.

"I didn't play well enough because I didn't work hard enough," Watson said of his slump in an Associated Press article. But he vowed to work harder, and he had tied for third at Pebble Beach and Hawaii heading into the Masters.

With Nicklaus and Watson struggling, many vied to fill their roles as the leading Americans.

The list included:

- Former Masters champions Raymond Floyd, Fuzzy Zoeller, Craig Stadler, and Ben Crenshaw.
- Major champions Hale Irwin, Lee Trevino, Hubert Green, Larry Nelson, and Hal Sutton.
- Experienced players Lanny Wadkins, Curtis Strange, Tom Kite, Andy Bean, Calvin Peete, and Jim Thorpe.
- Promising youngsters Mark O'Meara, Corey Pavin, Payne Stewart, Larry Mize, and Fred Couples.

All of those players were in the top fifty of the Sony Ranking.

CHAPTER 6

Family Affair

For years, Jack Nicklaus had followed the same pattern of preparation for major tournaments. His rule was to not play in an event the week before one of the four majors. He would come to Augusta the week before and put in his practice rounds, then leave sometime over the weekend and return to Augusta on Tuesday of Masters Week.

Rather than wear himself out with tedious practice rounds under the scrutiny of the patrons, Nicklaus generally arrived with a fresh perspective. He made it back in time for some work on the course and to attend the Champions Dinner, and on Wednesdays he would spend some more time on the "big course" and range working on his game. He rarely played in the Par-3 Contest.

Most golfers rent big houses and take their families to the Masters, and Nicklaus was no exception. He also had some special company that year. His mother, Helen, made the trip to Augusta for the first time since he debuted in the Masters in 1959. And his sister Marilyn and her husband, Howdy Hutchinson, also were on hand for the week. Barbara Nicklaus said Jack's mother came up with the idea out of the "clear blue."

"She says, 'Jack, there's only one thing I want to do. I'd like to go to one more Masters,'" Barbara recalled.

The Nicklaus party split into two houses: Jack, Barbara, and Jackie, along with two couples who were close friends, stayed at a house not far from Augusta National. Helen Nicklaus, Marilyn, and Howdy all rented a house in Reynolds Plantation, about halfway between Augusta and Atlanta.

"Of course they came over to our house every night, and we sat around and I played the piano and we sang. It was just a fabulous family week," Barbara said.

Who knew the Golden Bear could also sing?

"I'm playing the piano, and he's attempting to sing," Barbara said with a laugh. "But it was just one of those weeks that kind of fell into being perfect."

Nicklaus's father, Charlie, had died in 1970. Helen and Charlie had accompanied Nicklaus on his first trip to Augusta National as an amateur, and had stayed in the old Bon Air Hotel while Nicklaus slept in the Crow's Nest above the clubhouse.

"It was an exciting week for me and for the family," Nicklaus said. "I think the neatest part of that week was, in my opinion, having my friend Jack on the bag and having my mother there. It was the first time she had actually been to the Masters since I was a pro. She was on the first year when I was an amateur. And I don't know why but she said she wanted to go back one more time and she did. And my sister, I think—I'm not certain—I think it was my sister's first time ever in Augusta. And why she picked that year I don't know, maybe it was the year because my mother went too. So it was kind of nice, turned out to be a nice family affair."

Of Jack and Barbara's five children, only Jackie made it to Augusta in 1986. Daughter Nan was visiting friends while on spring break, and son Steve was working at the PGA Tour event in Hattiesburg, Mississippi. The two youngest children, Gary and Michael, stayed home in Florida.

Jackie, the oldest Nicklaus child, was serving as caddie for the first time at the Masters.

In his five Masters victories, Nicklaus used Augusta National caddie Willie Peterson to carry his bag. But when the Masters rescinded the rule that players must use local caddies, Nicklaus started branching out. He used a different one in 1984 and 1985, and decided on Jackie for 1986.

Both Jackie and second-oldest son Steve had caddied for their father before. He had won at Colonial with Steve on the bag in 1982, and he won his Memorial Tournament in 1984 with Jackie toting his clubs.

"It was just a point in my career where I wasn't having a permanent caddie anymore," Nicklaus said. "Jack and Steve were probably the best two caddies I ever had because they understand me and they understand what I do."

Jackie Nicklaus was first pressed into caddie duty at the 1976 British Open, when his father's regular caddie, Jimmy Dickinson, tore his Achilles'

(Above left) Jack Nicklaus and his caddie and son, Jackie, line up a putt on the 10th green. The younger Nicklaus had been the caddie for his father's last PGA Tour win at the 1984 Memorial Tournament, but 1986 was the first time Nicklaus had used his son as a caddie at the Masters. (Above right) Nicklaus and his son look over a putt in the third round. (Left) Nicklaus and Jackie study a birdie putt on the final hole. Nicklaus almost made the putt and left himself just a tap in for a round of 65.

tendon during a practice round. Fourteen-year-old Jackie took over the bag for the final nine holes.

"He hit a shot into the green and we started walking," Jackie said. "He said, 'Whoa. If you're the caddie, you've got to replace the divot.' It was a learning process."

At Augusta, the elder Nicklaus took his son to the caddie shack and got him set up. He was outfitted with the white coveralls that caddies wear—Jackie said they looked like something the "Good Humor Man" would wear—and he started fitting in.

"We'd eat fried pork sandwiches on even days and fried chicken on odd days, two pieces of Wonder bread and a squirt of mustard," Jackie said.

While the focus of the media and fans was on Ballesteros, Langer, and Norman, Nicklaus was able to go about his preparations. Gone were the days of Nicklaus merely showing up and being the favorite.

Nicklaus had long said that he would never be a ceremonial golfer, but others weren't so sure. Could a 46-year-old really contend in a major? Nicklaus had always vowed that he would stop competing when he felt he no longer had a chance to win. Merely showing up was not enough for him.

In an article that ran in Tuesday's *Augusta Chronicle* under the headline Masters Serves as Test for Nicklaus, Associated Press golf writer Bob Green questioned whether Nicklaus's game was up for the challenge of the Masters.

"Can he again play at a high, competitive level the game he dominated for two decades?" Green wrote. "Will this proud man continue to play if he cannot perform at the level he demands of himself?"

Nicklaus said that he still enjoyed playing competitively. "But, obviously, I don't enjoy playing golf the way I've played it this year," he said.

He admitted that his focus was lacking for regular events, but hinted that he might devote more practice time for the majors. "Depending on what happens, I may play only four or five more times the rest of the year," Nicklaus said.

Nicklaus's first practice round that week did little to boost his confidence. On a rainy afternoon, he played with three amateurs: University of

Jack Nicklaus takes a club from his caddie and son, Jackie, during Tuesday's practice round at the 1986 Masters.

Georgia golfer Peter Persons, Persons's former teammate Chip Drury, and British Amateur champ Garth McGimpsey of Northern Ireland.

Persons had written Nicklaus ahead of time and asked for a practice round, and Nicklaus had obliged. The amateur from Macon, Georgia, put on the performance of his young life, turning in 35, and then he made eagle at 15 and birdie at 16. He wound up with 5-under 67, which trumped the Golden Bear's unofficial score of 74.

"It doesn't make any difference what he shot," Persons told the *Atlanta Journal*. "Shoot, I'm pulling for him more than I am myself, I think."

CHAPTER 7

Down to Business

Jack Nicklaus was having problems on the golf course in 1986. Rumors of problems off the course were swirling around him in 1986, too.

Nicklaus had a few marketing and endorsement relationships, but his business focus was primarily centered on his burgeoning golf course design firm. By the mid-1980s he was well on his way to commanding nearly $1 million for a signature design.

But two golf courses with real estate ties, St. Andrews in New York and Bear Creek in California, turned sour in 1985.

"That was a press thing. We were having some issues as it related to Bear Creek and St. Andrews," Nicklaus said. "Heck, I had been through other issues before. I just happened to be going through those issues at that time. It really had nothing to do with my company."

One person who had to broach the subject with Nicklaus was Rick Reilly. The acclaimed writer and columnist had just joined *Sports Illustrated*, and on his first trip to the Masters he was told to ask Nicklaus about his problems.

"I remember being scared to death—I had just been hired—and I remember on Wednesday I had to go up to Jack Nicklaus, who I had never met," Reilly recalled. "We had this whole story that had to be reported. I said 'Jack, I'm Rick Reilly.' Trembling. He's just about to go in the Champions Locker Room. I had never even seen the place. I said, 'Jack, we hear you're broke.' The words would barely get out of my mouth. And he said, 'Oh, not exactly.' I got to go in the Champions Locker Room, and he tried to explain it to me that he was overleveraged and he wasn't broke. It was scary as hell."

While other golfers usually warmed up for the tournament by playing in the Par-3 Contest, Nicklaus always held a pre-tournament interview in the afternoon after a practice round on the big course. Jack Berry of the *Detroit*

News, who was president of the Golf Writers Association of America, said the decision to come to the press building was not entirely up to Nicklaus.

"I was asked at the beginning of the week by one of the Yates brothers [Charles and Dan, who were on the tournament's press committee] if we [the writers] wanted Jack in for a pre-tournament interview," Berry said. "I said no, that we didn't want to embarrass him. He had played godawful that year prior to the Masters and he was 46 years old. No chance. Ancient. So he wasn't invited in for an interview."

Nicklaus played a practice round and signed autographs for dozens of fans as he made his way from the 18th green to the clubhouse area. Nicklaus did talk to the press that afternoon in an informal scrum, and the *Chronicle*'s Robert Naddra was one of the reporters who caught up with him.

Nicklaus admitted that he had been distracted and that he was ready to focus on golf again. "I took over my own business back in September. I've never been involved in it in that magnitude before so golf really hasn't been my No. 1 priority over the past six months," Nicklaus said. "But with the Masters coming up and the major championship season here, golf will be my No. 1 priority now."

With his new, oversized putter, Nicklaus said his game was coming along fine. "My chances are better than they were a week or two ago," he said. "I didn't think too much of my chances then."

Although Nicklaus's recent performances left something to be desired, his peers weren't ready to write him off. "I think he can still win it," Greg Norman said. "He's still got the nerve—maybe not as much as he once had—but he's still got it. Nobody's going to lose it that fast."

Tom Kite agreed. "To say he's not going to be a factor in any tournament would be very foolish," Kite said. "But he would have to play very well."

Glenn Sheeley, writing an article on Nicklaus's chances in the *Atlanta Constitution,* said the Golden Bear's game was not quite ready for prime time. "It's time for Carnegie Hall and he's having difficulty hitting all the right notes at the town band shell," Sheeley wrote.

Even CBS analyst Ken Venturi, who knew a thing or two about the Masters, took issue with the state of Nicklaus's game. Venturi was a two-time runner-up at Augusta. "I haven't seen him play because he hasn't been

Gary Koch won the Par-3 Contest in a playoff against Larry Mize. No winner of the Par-3 Contest has ever won the Masters in the same year, and Koch kept the tradition alive by finishing tied for 16th.

around to be on the air," Venturi said in Sheeley's article. "Jack's got to start thinking about when it is time [to retire]."

Even if Nicklaus was not holding court in the press room, there was plenty of action to report on. The morning of April 9th belonged to the chairman's annual "State of the Masters" address, and the afternoon focus was on the Par-3 Contest.

The Par-3 Contest required extra holes to be decided. Gary Koch and former Augustan Larry Mize each shot 4-under 23, and Koch prevailed on the third hole of a sudden-death playoff when he rolled in a 25-foot birdie putt.

Koch was well aware of the Par-3 jinx—no winner of that competition has ever won the Masters in the same year—but said it would help him. "It is just the Par-3 tournament, but a putt like that can boost your confidence," he said.

If Nicklaus was ready to pass the torch, Seve Ballesteros was ready to take the flame and run with it. He celebrated his 29th birthday by talking to the press and, on the eve of the tournament, declared that the 50th tournament "is mine."

Those were strong words for a golfer who had been banished from the PGA Tour in a dispute over the number of tournaments players were required to tee it up in. Ballesteros had only played once on the PGA tour before the Masters, and that was a missed cut in New Orleans.

"The lack of competition won't make any difference," Ballesteros said. "Yes, I feel ready to win. I'm ready. I'm talking serious. Of course, you can't be 100 percent, but I'm ready."

In a bold prediction, Ballesteros said the tournament would be over by the time he reached the 16th tee on Sunday.

"It will be over by then . . . I win," Ballesteros said.

CHAPTER 8

Opening Day

Ken Green and the Masters weren't a match made in heaven.

Augusta National is golf's cathedral, a place where decorum is required; Ken Green was a free spirit who once smuggled buddies into the Masters in the trunk of his car.

Augusta National's members are genteel; Green was anything but genteel, and he once ordered a beer, and drank it, while playing the 15th hole with Arnold Palmer at the Masters.

The Masters required that golfers use club caddies up until 1983; Green brought his sister, Shelley, to carry his bag in 1986, and she was one of the first female caddies in tournament history.

Green claimed that he started the tradition of skipping balls across the pond at No. 16 in practice rounds, but his antics usually resulted in penalties. "I was probably fined more times at the Masters than at any other event; I was fined at least once for every event I played, and twice once," Green told the *Augusta Chronicle* in 2010.

There was nothing to suggest that Green, a Masters rookie, could be a factor. But Green and journeyman Bill Kratzert each shot 4-under-par 68s to take the lead on opening day, April 10, 1986.

So much for European domination.

After rain earlier in the week, the golf course firmed up as winds up to 25 mph swept through Augusta National. Only two other players, T. C. Chen and Gary Koch, were able to break 70. Chen and Koch shot 69s and trailed by one.

Green made several long putts to highlight his round. "What can I say? So I made a few putts, four or five no-brainers," Green told reporters after his round.

LEADERBOARD

FIRST ROUND

THURSDAY, APRIL 10

POSITION	PLAYER	FRONT NINE	BACK NINE	TOTAL STROKES
T1	KEN GREEN	33	35	68
T1	BILL KRATZERT	35	33	68
T3	GARY KOCH	35	34	69
T3	T.C. CHEN	37	32	69
T5	DAVE BARR	37	33	70
T5	TOMMY NAKAJIMA	35	35	70
T5	BOB TWAY	37	33	70
T5	TOM KITE	36	34	70
T5	TOM WATSON	35	35	70
T5	GREG NORMAN	36	34	70
T25	JACK NICKLAUS	37	37	74

His birdies included a 40-footer at No. 1, 70 feet at No. 5, 40-plus feet at No. 16, and 35 feet at No. 18.

Kratzert also made his share of lucky putts, including a 60-footer on the first hole that set the tone for his day. "That gave me the confidence I needed on the rest of the greens," Kratzert said.

Green might not have been a regular at the Masters, but he was a hit in the press building with his quotes. "I am not an unknown. I am not a quiet clone," Green was quoted as saying in Roger Whiddon's lead in the next day's *Augusta Chronicle*. "I do have color. Everyone in my family knows me."

Like Green, Kratzert also was using an inexperienced caddie. He had released his regular caddie the day before the tournament and was using a friend from his hometown of Fort Wayne, Indiana.

(Left) Ken Green blasts out of a bunker en route to a first-round 68 at the 1986 Masters. Green, who was playing in his first Masters, made several long putts to share the lead with Bill Kratzert. (Below) Green brought his sister Shelley to caddie for him at the 1986 Masters. The Masters allowed players to bring their own caddies beginning in 1983, ending the tradition of using only Augusta National caddies.

Bill Kratzert watches a chip shot during the 1986 Masters. Kratzert shot 4-under 68 in the opening round and shared the lead with Ken Green.

Kratzert picked up birdies at the 13th, 15th, and 17th holes to come home in 3-under 33.

The greens were the other story of Thursday's play. Several players commented on the slick surfaces after their rounds.

"Never played greens like these," said Chen, who was best known for his infamous "two-chip" penalty the year before at the U.S. Open. "Sometimes, even 8 to 10 feet, I think two-putt."

Defending champion Bernhard Langer had a tough day on the greens. "The greens were so fast, you couldn't stop the ball," said Langer, who opened with 74. "It kept going, going and going."

Tom Kite, whose experience at the Masters dated back to the early 1970s, declared that Augusta National's greens were the fastest he'd ever seen. "The wind, coupled with the speed of the greens, made it incredible," he said.

Still, several of the big names managed to stay within striking distance. Tom Watson, Greg Norman, and Kite were among those who shot 70, and the contingent at 71 included former winners Seve Ballesteros and Ben Crenshaw.

Jack Nicklaus was among those who didn't fare as well in the opening round.

The five-time winner teed off in the afternoon and was paired with amateur Scott Verplank. Nicklaus made bogey at the par-4 third after a wild slice that saw his ball wind up in the second fairway, and he made the turn in 1-over 37.

On the second nine, Nicklaus made bogeys at Nos. 11 and 12 before making his first birdie of the day at the par-5 13th. He made par on the remaining holes to complete a 37 for a total of 2-over 74.

Ben Crenshaw looks down after hitting a shot in the 1986 Masters. Crenshaw tied for 16th after shooting a final-round 70.

Jack Nicklaus hits out of a bunker in the first round of the 1986 Masters. Nicklaus had been struggling that year, and his 74 left him well behind the leaders.

Despite his newfangled MacGregor Response ZT putter, Nicklaus struggled on the greens. He required thirty-five putts, and he missed four birdie tries that were inside 15 feet. He drove the ball well and hit fourteen greens in regulation, but was clearly frustrated by the 74.

The *Chronicle* pointed out that it was only the second time since 1963 that Nicklaus had opened the Masters with a score higher than 73. Nicklaus had actually started to feel good about his game, but those feelings disappeared.

"I was really down on myself for shooting 74 because I played pretty well but I didn't make any putts," Nicklaus said. "I didn't putt very well."

CHAPTER 9

Making the Cut

The second round of the Masters was just as eventful as the first.

Bill Kratzert, the veteran, held steady. Ken Green, the rookie, faded. And Seve Ballesteros, the favorite, charged into the lead.

Several big names failed to make the thirty-six-hole cut, which fell at 5-over-par 149. Those included former champions Arnold Palmer, Gary Player, Raymond Floyd, and Craig Stadler.

Ballesteros grabbed the headlines with a round of 68 that included four birdies and an eagle. Earlier in the week, the young Spaniard was quoted as saying he was ready to win the tournament. After his performance on Friday, April 11th, he backed away from those comments. "I was misinterpreted," he said. "I want to make perfectly clear, right now, I'd never say that."

During his session with the press, according to Dan Jenkins's report in *Golf Digest*, the subject of Ballesteros's feud with PGA Tour commissioner Deane Beman came up again.

Jenkins wrote: "Of everyone involved, Ballesteros looked the most determined, the most dedicated, the player with the most motivation, having been banished from the American circuit for 1986 by the stubborn enforcement of a silly rule, or so growing numbers of fans, journalists and competitors are beginning to believe.

"After his Friday round, Ballesteros found himself in an exchange with the *Atlanta Journal*'s gifted columnist, Furman Bisher, a conversation worth repeating.

"Furman said, 'Seve, you played like you were on a crusade today. Are you trying to prove something to the PGA Tour?'

"Seve responded, 'Did Deane Beman pay you to ask that question?'

"Furman said, 'No, it's a legitimate question. Are you on a crusade?'

"'You talk too sophisticated for me,' said Seve. 'I don't understand.'

"'You ought to know what a crusade is,' Furman said. 'They started in Spain.'

"Seve didn't have a kicker line because like most everybody else in the press building, he'd never learned that the Crusades had actually started in Rome," Jenkins wrote.

History lessons aside, no one could dispute that the young Spaniard was playing wonderful golf. He made three birdies on the front nine against no bogeys, but he made bogey on the par-5 13th. He recovered with a 25-foot putt for eagle at the 15th. The fiery Ballesteros punctuated the eagle with a clenched fist.

LEADERBOARD

SECOND ROUND

FRIDAY, APRIL 11

POSITION	PLAYER	ROUND ONE	ROUND TWO	TOTAL STROKES
1	SEVE BALLESTEROS	71	68	139
2	BILL KRATZERT	68	72	140
3	TOMMY NAKAJIMA	70	71	141
T4	DANNY EDWARDS	71	71	142
T4	BEN CRENSHAW	71	71	142
T4	GREG NORMAN	70	72	142
T4	T.C. CHEN	69	73	142
T4	BERNHARD LANGER	74	68	142
T9	MARK MCCUMBER	76	67	143
T9	COREY PAVIN	71	72	143
T9	BOB TWAY	70	73	143
T9	GARY KOCH	69	74	143
T17	JACK NICKLAUS	74	71	145

Seve Ballesteros watches a putt during the second round of the 1986 Masters. Ballesteros shot 68 and seized the lead at the halfway mark of the tournament.

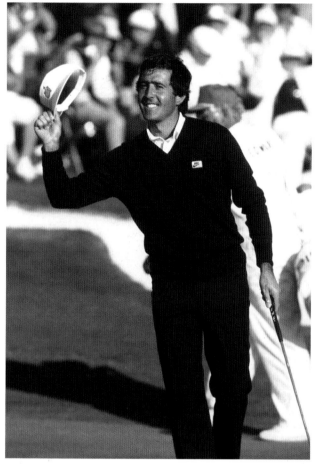

Seve Ballesteros tips his visor to the crowd after making birdie at the 18th hole in the second round of the 1986 Masters. The Spaniard held a one-shot lead over Bill Kratzert at the halfway point of the tournament.

"I don't have to prove anything," Ballesteros said. "If I win, great. If not, I'll be back next year."

Despite making a bogey at the 16th, Ballesteros wrapped up his 68 with a birdie on the final hole. His total of 5-under 139 put him one shot ahead of Kratzert, who toured Augusta National in even-par 72.

"I think I shot what I should've," Kratzert said. "I couldn't have got any more out of the round."

Green, meanwhile, did what most first-timers do after getting a lead at the Masters. He came back to earth. He soared to a 41 on the front nine and came home in 37 for a 78, ten shots worse than his opening round.

"I played like your basic 12-handicapper," Green quipped. "I wasn't nervous, but my swing was too quick."

Japan's Tommy Nakajima was alone in third after shooting a 1-under 71 that included an eagle on his nemesis, the par-5 13th. "It is my friend," Nakajima told reporters. "I feel I have more than redeemed myself for that one bad day."

Defending champion Bernhard Langer switched to a lighter putter for the second round and found it to his liking. He made five birdies against one bogey in his round of 68.

With Langer, Greg Norman, and T. C. Chen also in the top ten, the 50th Masters was shaping up as a foreign affair.

Ken Green squats down as he watches a putt during the 1986 Masters. After shooting 68 in the first round, Green came back to earth with a 78 in the second round.

"The foreign players' names are in red and there's five of them among the first eight names on the leaderboard," Al Ludwick wrote in his column in the *Chronicle*. "It's enough to make your American blood boil if you think too much about it."

Jack Nicklaus blasts out of a bunker during the second round of the 1986 Masters. Nicklaus shot 1-under 71 to make the thirty-six-hole cut and keep his hopes of winning alive.

At one point Friday afternoon, seven of the top ten spots were occupied by foreign players. Atlanta writer Glenn Sheeley recalled a funny line from a St. Petersburg–based columnist that was heard by only a few in the press building.

"Hubert Mizell said this wouldn't happen if Jack Nicklaus were alive," Sheeley said. "It got a nice laugh from the people around him."

Nicklaus was very much alive, even if his golf game had yet to fire on all cylinders. Nicklaus made the cut with room to spare after shooting 1-under 71. Playing with Jim Thorpe, his round was fairly quiet as he carded three birdies to offset two bogeys.

After the round, Nicklaus again lamented his woes on the putting green. In the first two days, Nicklaus said, he had twenty-three putts inside of 15 feet. But he only made five of those, even though he switched to a new over-sized putter before the tournament.

"When you have the ball that close that many times, you have to make more putts," Nicklaus said in the *Chronicle*. "I made one yesterday and made [three] on this round. We're talking makeables, whether for par or birdie."

Still, with only six shots separating him from Ballesteros and the lead, Nicklaus saw a glimmer of hope.

"I'm not satisfied with 74-71. I've played the best two rounds of the year and haven't scored," he said. "I feel like I did play pretty well. I'm finally playing like that fellow I used to know."

CHAPTER 10

Moving Day

Augusta National was a course built for scoring. Unlike U.S. Open layouts that featured thick rough and narrow fairways, Augusta National was relatively open and lacking much rough. Its main defense was its greens, which were enormous, full of slopes, and lightning quick.

It's ironic that when Augusta National co-founders Bobby Jones and Clifford Roberts opened the course in the early 1930s, their first goal was to hold a U.S. Open. When that was shot down because of Augusta's summer climate and logistical issues, they settled on a springtime event that evolved into the Masters.

Jones, in the description of Augusta National he penned for *Sports Illustrated* in 1959, wrote that "we are quite willing to have low scores made during the tournament. It is not our intention to rig the golf course so as to make it tricky."

Furthermore, Jones wrote: "We want to make the bogies easy if frankly sought, pars readily obtainable by standard good play, and birdies, except on the par 5s, dearly bought."

And he was right. The course yielded plenty of scores in the 60s in the early years, and in 1940 Lloyd Mangrum set the benchmark with his 8-under 64 in the opening round. It was twenty-five years before anyone matched that mark, but Jack Nicklaus did in 1965.

Maurice Bembridge (1974), Hale Irwin (1975), Gary Player (1978), and Miller Barber (1979) had all shot 64s in the years after Nicklaus. But no one had broken the record established by Mangrum nearly fifty years earlier.

Enter Nick Price, a lanky pro from Zimbabwe who had only played in one previous Masters, in 1984, and had missed the cut. His biggest moment in golf had come when he was runner-up to Tom Watson at the 1982 British Open.

Price wasn't among the favorites at Augusta, and his opening 79 featured "six or seven" three-putt greens. "I was really frustrated. I was hitting the ball well enough to compete, but I just wasn't putting well enough," Price said.

Some extra work on the putting green helped Price shoot 69 in the second round, and he made the cut of 5-over 149 by one shot.

On Saturday, April 12, 1986, conditions for the third round at Augusta National were relatively benign, and Price had an opportunity to move up the leaderboard if he could post a decent score. So he promptly went out and hit his opening tee shot in the fairway bunker, and bogeyed the first hole. "And then I probably had the best 17 holes of putting I've ever had," Price said.

He birdied the second hole. Then the fifth, sixth, and eighth. Price made the turn in 3-under 33, and that's when he really got hot.

The 29-year-old made birdies on the next four holes, which included all three holes of Amen Corner. That put him at 7-under for the day and well within range of the course record of 8-under 64.

"What I suppose I remember the best was walking up the 14th hole, and I think at this stage I was 7 under, and saying to my caddie do you know what the course record is," Price said. "And he nodded at me and said, 'Yeah.' And I said, 'Let's do it.'"

Price made birdies at the 15th and 16th holes to reach 9-under for his round, and his birdie putt on the 17th ran over the top edge of the cup. On the final hole, Price's lengthy birdie putt found a good piece of the cup but didn't fall. Dan Jenkins, writing in *Golf Digest*, quipped that Price "had a 'margarita' on the 18th, a birdie putt that rimmed the entire cup but stayed out."

Price knew the 63 was rare territory, and he joked afterward that Augusta National's founding father had had enough. "They were asking what happened on that 18th hole and I came up with this line," Price said. "I think Bobby Jones' hand came up and popped it out the hole. And said, 'That's enough.'"

With ten birdies against just one bogey, Price had vaulted into contention. His 5-under total through fifty-four holes left him one shot behind leader Greg Norman, who had shot 4-under 68.

(Above left) Nick Price and his caddie look over a putt during the third round of the 1986 Masters. (Above right) Nick Price celebrates after tapping in his par putt for a course record 9-under 63. After making bogey on the first hole, Price fired ten birdies to break the course record held by six other golfers. (Left) Nick Price—and the gallery at the 18th hole—can't believe his birdie putt didn't fall in the third round of the 1986 Masters. Price's record score stood for ten years until it was matched by his good friend, Greg Norman, in the opening round of the 1996 Masters.

Greg Norman took the lead after three rounds of the 1986 Masters with rounds of 70, 72, and 68. Norman held the lead after fifty-four holes in all four majors that year, but only won the British Open.

The Great White Shark had caught fire on the second nine with four birdies to take the lead. Labeled the "Next Nicklaus" by many for his powerful game and shock of whitish-blond hair, Norman had yet to win a major. But he had contended at Augusta before, and most figured it was just a matter of time before he slipped on a green jacket.

Norman seized the lead by playing the final nine in 4-under 32, including birdies on all three holes of Amen Corner. He birdied the 17th hole to complete his 68.

On a course with many temptations for a long-hitter, Norman said he was exercising patience. "In the past, I've always been too aggressive here," Norman said in the *Chronicle*. "I've changed my line of thinking. I played every shot in practice just like I would in the tournament, either lay up or hit for the center of the fairway."

LEADERBOARD

THIRD ROUND

SATURDAY, APRIL 12

POSITION	PLAYER	ROUND ONE	ROUND TWO	ROUND THREE	TOTAL STROKES
1	GREG NORMAN	70	72	68	210
T2	BERNHARD LANGER	74	68	69	211
T2	SEVE BALLESTEROS	71	68	72	211
T2	NICK PRICE	79	69	63	211
T2	DONNIE HAMMOND	73	71	67	211
T6	TOM KITE	70	74	68	212
T6	TOMMY NAKAJIMA	70	71	71	212
T6	TOM WATSON	70	74	68	212
T9	SANDY LYLE	76	70	68	214
T9	DANNY EDWARDS	71	71	72	214
T9	BOB TWAY	70	73	71	214
T9	GARY KOCH	69	74	71	214
T9	COREY PAVIN	71	72	71	214
T9	MARK MCCUMBER	76	67	71	214
T9	JACK NICKLAUS	74	71	69	214

Ballesteros must have felt like he was being lapped by the field with his round of even-par 72. As Price set a course record and Norman and others scored in the 60s, the Spaniard bogeyed his final two holes and relinquished his lead.

"I like my position, but not the way I finished," said Ballesteros, who blamed a cold putter for his scoring woes. "Maybe I was just saving my putts for tomorrow."

First-round co-leader Bill Kratzert soared to a 76 and was out of the running. The former University of Georgia star stumbled with six bogeys against only two birdies.

Bill Kratzert acknowledges the crowd after making a putt at the 1986 Masters. Kratzert shot rounds of 68 and 72, but faded from contention on the weekend with scores of 76 and 79.

Donnie Hammond, a tournament rookie who had served as a gallery guard for the 1975 Masters, shot 5-under 67 and leaped into a tie for second place. Instead of concentrating on finishing in the top twenty-four to get a return invitation, Hammond began to entertain thoughts of winning. The last first-timer to win was Fuzzy Zoeller in 1979.

"I feel super about my position with one round to go," Hammond said. "I just hope I can keep my putter hot. If I do, I have a shot at winning."

Jack Nicklaus, meanwhile, put himself into contention. Paired with Jay Haas, he turned in 34, then made birdies at Nos. 11 and 12 to make a move of his own. But his momentum was derailed when he found the tributary of Rae's Creek at No. 13, and he walked away with a disappointing bogey.

A par at the par-5 15th also was a setback. Still, his 69 put him at 2-under for the tournament and four behind Norman.

Jack Nicklaus watches a putt during the third round of the 1986 Masters. Nicklaus shot 69 to move into the top ten and put himself in striking distance of leader Greg Norman.

"I'm kind of unhappy with 13 and 15," Nicklaus said in the *Atlanta Journal-Constitution*. "I mean, I bogey 13 and par 15. Two birdies there and I'm 5-under par [for the tournament]. A big difference. I'd be a lot happier then. But good gracious, I can't remember the last time I broke 70."

The problem for Nicklaus was not the deficit, but how many golfers stood between him and Norman. Price, Ballesteros, Hammond, and Bernhard Langer were at 5-under and one shot behind Norman, and Tom Kite, Tom Watson, and Tommy Nakajima were all at 4-under for the tournament.

Six other players, including Sandy Lyle, were tied with Nicklaus for ninth place. The Golden Bear, though, refused to concede the tournament. "I would assume I'm close enough to be in the hunt," he said in the *Chronicle*. "Anytime you're in Augusta, it's the number of players rather than the shots. Certainly where I am is in pretty good shape."

Nicklaus then made one final prediction.

"I've been playing considerably better. I should've been better than 69 today," Nicklaus said. "If I keep playing the way I'm playing, make a few putts, I might scare somebody."

CHAPTER 11

The Front Nine

The key pairings for the final round:
    1:16 p.m.: Mark McCumber, Corey Pavin
    1:24 p.m.: Bob Tway, Gary Koch
    1:32 p.m.: Sandy Lyle, Jack Nicklaus
    1:40 p.m.: Tom Watson, Tommy Nakajima
    1:48 p.m.: Seve Ballesteros, Tom Kite
    1:56 p.m.: Donnie Hammond, Bernhard Langer
    2:04 p.m.: Greg Norman, Nick Price

On the morning of Sunday, April 13, 1986, Jack Nicklaus woke up to a perfect Augusta day. Sunny skies. A gentle breeze. A day perfect for scoring. And an article taped to his refrigerator that said he couldn't win.

Nicklaus took a call from his second-oldest son, Steve. He was working at the PGA Tour event in Hattiesburg, Mississippi, commonly referred to as the "Mississippi Masters" because of its spot on the schedule.

"What do you think, Pops?" Nicklaus remembered Steve asking. "I said 'Steve, I think 66 will tie and 65 will win. What do you think?' He said that's the exact number I had in mind. Go shoot it."

Despite the family support, there was little evidence to make a case for the Golden Bear to win his eighteenth professional major. He hadn't won in two years, and he hadn't really contended in a major since the 1983 PGA. His last hurrah in Augusta had been five years before, and he wound up tied for second as Tom Watson won another major at his expense.

Of the eight golfers ahead of Nicklaus entering the final round, two-time Masters winners Watson and Ballesteros stood out as the biggest favorites to win. Langer had one major, the previous year's Masters, to his credit.

Norman, Price, Hammond, Kite, and Nakajima had yet to win a major, but all hoped to slip into a green jacket by the end of the day.

Nicklaus arrived in front of Augusta National's clubhouse and greeted well-wishers before making his way to the Champions Locker Room. Wearing checkered pants, a yellow shirt, and a blue sweater vest, Nicklaus was relaxed.

Nicklaus wasn't scheduled to tee off until 1:32 p.m., so he took his time as he went through his usual warmup routine. Around 1:15, he and caddie-son Jackie arrived at the practice putting green not far from the first tee.

Jackie reached into the big green and white MacGregor golf bag and pulled out three new white golf balls. His father went about his business of chipping and practice putting.

With his tee time near, Nicklaus made his way to the first tee. By now the gallery size had increased considerably, and Nicklaus signed a few more autographs as he made the short walk.

Larry Mize teed off exactly two hours before Nicklaus. The Augusta native had worked on the leaderboards at the Masters as a kid and idolized Nicklaus. Qualifying for the 1984 Masters, and then earning return trips in 1985 and 1986, were certainly high on his list of achievements.

Mize didn't fit the bill as a Masters favorite. He wasn't long off the tee, and his game was steady but not spectacular. Making pars, not eagles, was his style.

Two weeks before the Masters, Mize had been in position to claim his biggest win since joining the PGA Tour in 1982. He shot three rounds in the 60s at the Tournament Players Championship, but he carded a 76 in the final round and finished second.

The hangover of that disappointment followed Mize to Augusta, where he shot rounds of 75, 74, and 72 leading into Sunday.

With ideal conditions—warm weather and little wind—and Sunday pin placements that were conducive to low scores, Mize took advantage. He made birdies at Nos. 2 and 6 and made the turn in 2-under-par 34. But if he was going to jump into the top twenty-four and secure a trip back to Augusta in 1987, he'd need to play some special golf on the final nine holes. "The back nine is where you make up the ground," Mize told the *Augusta Chronicle*.

Larry Mize tips his visor after completing a final-round 65 at the 1986 Masters. The score put Mize into the top sixteen, and enabled him to earn a return trip to the Masters. The Augusta native made the most of it and won the 1987 Masters in a sudden-death playoff with Greg Norman and Seve Ballesteros.

After pars at 10 and 11, Mize rolled in a 10-footer for birdie at 12. On the par-5 13th, he laid up short of the green and then hit an indifferent wedge to about 20 feet beyond the hole. "I didn't hit a very good wedge shot there but I told my caddie I was going to make it anyway," Mize said.

He did just that, and it set off an explosion of birdies. Mize made birdies at 14, 16, and 17 and, thanks to fine iron play, all of those putts were 10 feet or less.

Mize's 65 had proved that Augusta National was there for the taking, especially the second nine. But he was the only one of the early starters to make a move. Mize had started the day eleven shots behind Norman. But his 65 would move him all the way to a tie for 16th and earn him an invitation to the next year's Masters.

"You never want to think you're out of it, but I was eleven shots back," Mize said. "I definitely was thinking more to the top twenty-four."

Despite the optimal scoring conditions, none of the top eight made much of a move on the first nine holes.

Watson made no birdies and shot 1-over 37, while Nakajima birdied the second, but dropped shots at Nos. 4 and 6 to also shoot 37.

Kite didn't make a par until the fourth hole with two bogeys and a birdie to start his round. He vaulted into contention when he pitched in for an eagle at the par-5 8th to shoot 1-under 35. Ballesteros made par on his first six holes, then made birdie on the seventh. After Kite holed his third shot at No. 8, Ballesteros matched his eagle with a chip-in of his own. His 34 was the best front nine of the challengers.

Hammond, the former Masters gallery guard, suffered the worst front nine. He bogeyed four of the first seven holes to shoot 40 and drop out of contention. Langer birdied the second hole to pull into a tie with Norman, but fell back with bogeys at Nos. 7 and 8 to card a 37.

Price couldn't match the momentum of the day before and could make only one birdie, at the fourth, on the front nine. Two bogeys dropped him to 1-over 37. Norman, the fifty-four-hole leader, played the steadiest golf. He picked up only one birdie, at the sixth, but parred the rest for a 35.

Like the rest of the challengers, Nicklaus was treading water and not picking up any ground. After a par at the first, Nicklaus pushed his tee shot into the trees right of the second fairway. He pitched out into the fairway and then hit a nifty third shot to short range for a birdie. But he gave it back when he three-putted the fourth hole.

Nicklaus hit a terrific tee shot on the sixth, no more than 4 feet from the hole, to give him a great opportunity to pick up a shot. But his putter betrayed him again, and his gallery groaned its disapproval.

At the par-5 8th, Nicklaus reached back for a little extra and hit a big tee shot, but he pushed it and his ball wound up in a stand of pine trees. Still, he was within distance of reaching the green if he could find a way through it. The Golden Bear hadn't won his majors by taking uncalculated risks. He let others make unforced errors, and he always played it safe.

But this time his hand was forced. If he wanted a par or a birdie he had to play a gutsy shot between two of the pines, and if he had nicked one of them his ball could have caromed just about anywhere.

He selected a 6-foot gap between two pines, and took out his 3-wood. But he said he slipped slightly, and pushed his ball right of the target area. Somehow, the ball made its way through a gap about a foot wide and wound up right of the green. A female patron said that shot alone was worth the $75 price of admission.

"If my ball had caught one of those trees, I might still be there," Nicklaus later told *Golf Digest.*

Donnie Hammond vaulted into contention with a 67 in the third round of the 1986 Masters. A former gallery guard at the Masters, Hammond was making his tournament debut that year. Fuzzy Zoeller, in 1979, was the last first-time participant to win.

Nicklaus pitched to about 10 feet, but again his putter was cold. He walked away with par, but it could have been much worse.

Time was beginning to run out, and Nicklaus went to the ninth. After a perfect drive and splendid approach, he stood over a slippery 12-foot birdie putt at the 9th he knew he needed to make something happen.

Before Nicklaus could attempt his putt, though, he had to back off as a huge roar erupted behind him. "And I was getting ready to putt the ball and a big roar goes up from eight," Nicklaus said.

It was for Kite, who had just pitched in for eagle on the eighth from about 80 yards out. Getting ready to try his putt once more, Nicklaus had to stop again.

"All of a sudden another big roar goes off and the other one had hit the ball and knocked their third shot in the hole," Nicklaus said. This time it was for Ballesteros, who had topped Kite's eagle from just under 50 yards out.

"We both hit wedges," Kite said. "I hit it in first and he was right behind me."

Finally, there was some excitement. After about thirty minutes of boring golf, the action was starting to heat up. TV coverage began at 3 p.m., and coverage of the first nine holes was minimal.

The dueling eagles fired up Nicklaus, who turned to the gallery and issued a challenge. "I said, 'Hey, why don't we see if we can make a little noise up here ourselves.'"

Nicklaus finally settled over his putt, but not before some discussion with Jackie on the line. The son saw left edge. The father saw just outside the right edge.

They split the difference, and Nicklaus coaxed the birdie putt into the cup to make the turn in 1-under 35. At 3-under for the tournament, Nicklaus still trailed co-leaders Norman and Ballesteros by four shots. Kite was two ahead of him, and Price and Langer were one ahead.

"The interaction just completely energized my Dad," Jackie Nicklaus said. "Walking to the 10th tee, he had so many people shouting encouragement to him."

Nicklaus had cut down the number of challengers he had to pass, but his deficit was the same as when he started the day.

Could Nicklaus, at 46, overtake his younger competition and become the oldest Masters winner? Or were his clubs rusty and his game washed up?

The world was about to tune in.

CHAPTER 12

The Final Nine Begins: No. 10

There's a well-worn adage that says the Masters doesn't begin until the back nine on Sunday. Almost from the start, the tournament has had plenty of key moments occur in the final nine holes.

There was Gene Sarazen's double eagle at the 15th hole that enabled him to force a playoff, which he won, in 1935. There was Arnold Palmer's charge in 1960 with birdies on the final two holes to nip Ken Venturi, who could only watch. And, of course, Nicklaus won the famous battle with Tom Weiskopf and Johnny Miller in 1975. That tournament was defined by Nicklaus's 40-foot birdie putt at the 16th.

Who would slip into a green jacket late Sunday afternoon?

Would it be Ballesteros, the fiery Spaniard who had already proved he had the game to tame Augusta National?

Would it be Norman, the flashy Australian who had never won a major before but had challenged in his Masters debut?

Would it be Kite, the steady American who had blown a chance to win a green jacket two years earlier?

Would it be Langer, the stoic German who had overcome his history of putting woes to win the Masters a year earlier?

Would it be Price, the quiet South African who was finding out just how difficult it was to follow up a record round?

Or would it be Nicklaus, the master of Augusta who had not won here in more than a decade?

Not everyone connected to Nicklaus was watching intently as play on the final nine began.

Clay Long, head of research and development at MacGregor Golf and designer of the Response ZT putter, was at home in Albany, Georgia, that

**Final Round
Jack Nicklaus on the 10th Hole**

Par 4, 485 yards

   (1) Driver to right side of fairway
   (2) 4-iron to green
   (3) 25-foot putt for birdie

Jack Nicklaus looks on as his 25-foot birdie putt heads for the cup on the 10th hole. It was his second birdie in a row and would help Nicklaus play the final ten holes in 7-under par.

Sunday. With the tax filing deadline two days away, Long was filling out his forms and had the Masters telecast on in the background.

Nicklaus was coming off a birdie at the ninth, but he was still a long way from his target score of 6-under 66. With two reachable par-5s still in front of him, he knew a low score was possible. Now he just had to keep playing well and hope that a few putts would drop.

First up was the 10th, a downhill par-4 that yielded few birdies. Nicklaus pushed his tee shot a bit to the right, and it bounced off a male patron who quipped that he was glad it was on the bounce because it had hit him in a sensitive spot. "Good show," Nicklaus said when he arrived.

With a bit longer approach than he wanted, Nicklaus still hit a superb 4-iron shot into the green, and the ball settled about 25 feet from the hole. Nicklaus poured his ball into the middle of the cup. "I've got to believe that was the longest putt he made all week," Jackie said.

Two in a row, and now Nicklaus was 4-under and creeping toward the leaders. That's when Long started really paying attention to the telecast. "I was sitting there doing my taxes, looking over my shoulder and at some point I quit working on my taxes," Long said.

The switch to the new big-headed putter was paying dividends. After three frustrating rounds, Nicklaus had finally found some magic. This was exactly the kind of performance Long and the others involved with the putter's development had been waiting for. "It was big and you couldn't mishit it. It rolled the ball real good and the center of gravity was up," Long said.

With its bulky size, most people thought the Response ZT would be heavy. They were wrong, though. Long said the initial production was about C8 in swing weight.

Long said Nicklaus piled lead tape in the cavity of his putter—about eight or ten pieces —which made it about D2 in swing weight, which was standard for a putter.

"It put a great roll on the ball. You hit it solid every time," Long said. "If you made a bad stroke you couldn't tell it."

Long's phone started ringing soon after Nicklaus began his charge. "All my buddies were saying, 'Is that your putter?'" Long said.

Sandy Lyle, Nicklaus's playing partner, marveled at his control with the new putter. If the 46-year-old was feeling any nerves, he wasn't showing them. "That putter never trembled one minute. It was like it was coming out of a machine," Lyle said. "If you watched the putter head it was straight back, straight through. There was no toe overlapping the heel or whatever, or any kind of flinching. Just a man in control of his emotions. It was as pure as it gets."

CHAPTER 13

Amen Corner

Amen Corner is the most famous stretch of holes in golf, and it encompasses the 11th, 12th, and 13th holes at Augusta National.

It was given its nickname by Herbert Warren Wind, the famous golf writer who used the term to describe the decisive action in the 1958 Masters for his article in *Sports Illustrated*.

The 11th presents many challenges, including a tee shot out of a chute and a green that is guarded by a pond on the left. The safe route was to play to the right side of the green, or even miss it altogether and leave a short chip. Ben Hogan respected the hole so much that he once remarked that if you ever saw him on the green, you knew he missed his shot.

But this was no time for Nicklaus to play safe, and he cranked out a big drive that left him only an 8-iron for his approach. He hit it about 20 feet to the right, and it left him with a sweeping putt.

As the ball trickled toward the hole, CBS announcer Steve Melnyk excitedly called the action. "Is it enough, is it enough? Yes," Melnyk said. "Three birdies in a row for Nicklaus . . . 9, 10, and 11."

"I drained that putt and went, 'Whoops, that's pretty good,'" Nicklaus said. "I've made three in a row here now."

With the huge gallery at Amen Corner roaring its approval, folks around the course began to take notice of Nicklaus. "I think that was the first time I jumped," Jackie said in an interview for the tournament highlights tape. "I started getting really excited." He wasn't alone.

Nicklaus was starting to attract a crowd, and not just fans. Members of the press corps began to take an interest in what Nicklaus was doing. "When he birdied the ninth hole I thought maybe there was magic there. Then when the birdie string continued, it became a firestorm," said Ward Clayton, the golf writer for the *Durham Morning Herald*.

Final Round
Jack Nicklaus on the 11th Hole

Par 4, 455 yards

(1) Driver to right center of fairway
(2) 8-iron to green
(3) 20-foot putt for birdie

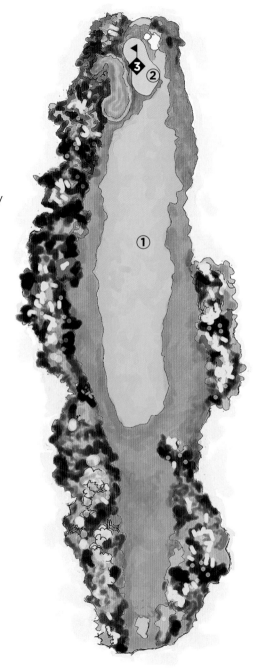

Jack Nicklaus and caddie Willie Peterson look on at the Masters during the 1970s. Peterson served as Nicklaus's caddie for his first five Masters wins in 1963, 1965, 1966, 1972, and 1975.

Clayton had been following Nicklaus on the front nine, along with longtime friend Buddy Whitfield and his family. "When Nicklaus made the birdie on nine, Buddy said it's time for a Budweiser. Buddy thought that was a good-luck charm because he thought a Budweiser was necessary after every birdie," Clayton recalled. "We didn't have the time, or the storage capacity, to order another Budweiser after Nicklaus made birdie on 11. We watched all the way to the finish."

Ron Green Jr., working for the *Greenville News*, also picked up Nicklaus at the turn and watched him through Amen Corner. He was struck by the fans who rushed to get a glimpse of Nicklaus. "I just remember hundreds of guys running down the hill [at 11] to catch up with him," Green said. "Something you don't really see there."

Rick Reilly of *Sports Illustrated* also noticed the lack of decorum. "That's the day the no running rule was totally violated. I mean women with heels were running," Reilly said. "People were abandoning their pimento cheese stations. Because you had to see it, you had to be there."

As Nicklaus made the short walk from the 11th green to the 12th tee, he was greeted by a thunderous ovation.

"That was probably the first time I noticed Dad getting emotional," Jackie said. "At that point, every time he approached a green or tee you could see him getting emotional, teary eyed, having to push back his emotions."

Among the thousands of patrons congregating in Amen Corner was Willie Peterson, Nicklaus's caddie for his five Masters wins. When after the 1982 tournament the Masters rescinded the rule that players must use Augusta National caddies, Peterson's days were numbered. But he was still loyal to his man, and as Nicklaus came to the 12th he offered a prediction. "If he shoots 30 (on the back nine), they can hang it up," Peterson told his buddies.

That was no hollow prediction. Peterson knew the ebb and flow of a Masters final round.

More importantly, he knew Nicklaus. The two had paired up when Nicklaus first came to Augusta National as an amateur in 1959. They had hit it off, and Peterson enjoyed the fame of being the caddie to the most successful golfer in Masters history.

Where Nicklaus was usually reserved in his celebrations, the outgoing Peterson was not. He would jump in the air when Nicklaus made a big putt, or he would thrust his arms in exultation.

He saved his biggest celebration for 1975, when Nicklaus rolled in a 40-foot birdie putt at the 16th. Peterson, who was tending the flagstick, jumped for joy as Nicklaus took off on a celebration of his own. The outburst, according to Dan Jenkins in *Sports Illustrated*, "made Nicklaus and his caddie, Willie Peterson, resemble Fred Astaire and Ginger Rogers."

**Final Round
Jack Nicklaus on the 12th Hole**

Par 3, 155 yards

(1) 7-iron over left side of green
(2) Chip to 6 feet
(3) and (4) Two putts for bogey

But that was eleven years ago. Even if others were reliving ancient history, Nicklaus had to focus on the task at hand.

The 12th hole might be the shortest at Augusta National, but golfers in the heat of a Sunday afternoon battle face no sterner test. With the pin set in its traditional location on the far right of the green, birdies are rare and pars are savored. With Rae's Creek flowing in front of the green, bunkers front and rear, and swirling winds, the slightest mistake can ruin a golfer's chance of winning the Masters.

With three birdies in a row, Nicklaus made the short walk from the 11th green to the 12th tee to a standing ovation. Nicklaus never took dead aim at the Sunday pin location, cut on the right side of the green and closest to Rae's Creek, and this year was no exception as he settled over the 162-yard shot.

He selected a 7-iron, and figured he would play for the fat of the green. But he tugged it left, and the ball wound up on the back fringe.

Chipping had never been one of Nicklaus's strong suits, but he felt he hit this one pretty good. But the ball took a funny bounce and wound up further away than Nicklaus expected.

Compounding matters was a spike mark directly between his ball and the cup. "I probably had more thought on the spike mark than I did on the putt," Nicklaus said. His par putt from 7 feet missed, and Nicklaus angrily stabbed his putter at the offending mark.

"It sort of brought me off of cloud nine, down to a place that was still pretty good, where I said, 'OK, I've played the last four holes in 2-under, and I've got a stretch coming up," Nicklaus said.

The bogey derailed his momentum, but it didn't knock Nicklaus out of contention. Behind him, Norman had found trouble at the 10th when he snap-hooked his tee shot on the dogleg left hole. The ball bounced back into the fairway, but Norman pulled his second shot well left of the green.

Price, Norman's playing partner, birdied the 10th to move up to 5-under. Kite, two groups behind Nicklaus, made birdie on the 11th to move to 6-under. Ballesteros, though, was playing the steadiest golf. After a bogey at the ninth, he made pars at Nos. 10 and 11.

CHAPTER 14

Back on Track

Rhett Sinclair had arrived to work his shift at the leaderboard on the 18th hole at about the same time Jack Nicklaus was teeing off in the final round.

The University of South Carolina—Aiken golfer had worked on Augusta National's famed leaderboards for the first time in 1984. He was stationed at the sixth hole, and he served there again in 1985.

In 1986, however, the outgoing Sinclair had moved up to the more visible location at the 18th hole. As the low man on the totem pole, Sinclair drew the task of climbing the ladder behind the hand-operated board and putting up numbers (red for under par, green for over par) to signify how each golfer stood in relation to par.

The 18th green was a favorite spot for patrons, and the board between the 18th and 10th fairways was situated so that the fans ringing the final hole's green could watch the action unfold. "That's their main source of keeping up with what's going on. You hear the roars and once we're posting a birdie on nine, a birdie on 10, and a birdie on 11 (for Nicklaus), everybody's starting to think, man, this guy can do it," Sinclair said.

Down at the 13th tee, Nicklaus prepared to shake off the bogey at the 12th and take on golf's ultimate risk-reward hole. At 465 yards, the par-5 13th has always been short by modern standards for a par-5.

Shape a drive around the bend in the dogleg, and you have a chance to attack the green and make birdie or eagle. If the drive is misplayed to the left, the tributary of Rae's Creek trickles down the fairway toward the green. If a golfer bails out right, a second shot from the pine needles is no bargain.

There was no question Nicklaus would attack this hole with his tee shot. Down three, time was becoming more of a factor. Nicklaus only had six holes left to make his move.

Final Round
Jack Nicklaus on the 13th Hole

Par 5, 465 yards

(1) 3-wood to left side of fairway
(2) 3-iron to green
(3) and (4) Two putts from 30
feet for birdie

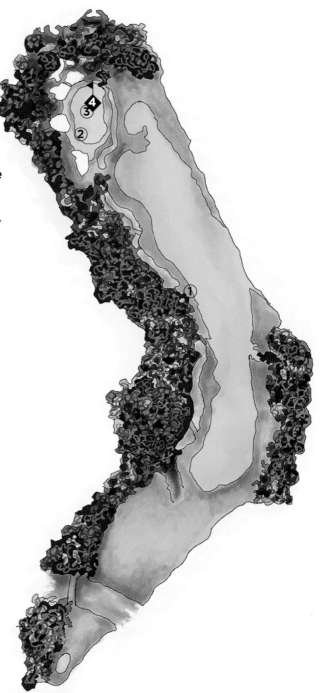

Nicklaus's tee shot was perfect. He hit a draw around the corner, and it flirted with the danger on the left side.

"He hit a drive on 13 and he pulled it a little bit and went over the edge of the trees but it did get out in the fairway," Jackie said in the highlights film. "I said 'Dad, that's not good on a 24-year-old heart.' He started laughing, thought that was pretty funny."

With just 210 yards to the pin, Nicklaus rifled a 3-iron shot toward the flag. The ball hit on the front of the green but checked up and left Nicklaus some 30 feet away. Nicklaus's eagle putt was on line, but it came up short and left him a short birdie putt. He tapped that in to move to 5-under.

The scorers at 13 radioed the information back to the scoring control center. From there, the message went out to each scoreboard to put a red 5 in the slot for Nicklaus at 13.

"When he birdied 13, when I held the door open and put the red number that showed the birdie, it was the first time the crowd at 18 started applauding," Sinclair said. "I started getting chills. Who wouldn't want Nicklaus to win at 46?"

Back on 10, Norman's woes continued. Earlier in the week, he had four-putted the green to suffer a double bogey. This time, with his second shot well left of the green, his third shot ran across the green and into the bunker. From there Norman took three more strokes to get into the cup. The double bogey put him at 5-under and gave Ballesteros sole possession of the lead.

By this time, golfers all around the country were tuned in to the telecast. The final round of the Masters was not to be missed. As the 46-year-old Nicklaus peeled off birdie after birdie, the level of interest grew.

"It was incredibly exciting. At all the golf courses around the country, guys played and came in to watch," Art Spander of the *San Francisco Chronicle* said. "Guys in their 40s and 50s. It was like they were reborn."

It wasn't just the old guys watching. In Southern California, a 10-year-old named Tiger Woods was glued to his television set. "I don't think I missed one minute of Sunday's round in 1986," Woods recalled. "The caliber of player Jack was, I can't say I was totally surprised, but it was an absolutely amazing performance. It seemed like he'd hit a spectacular shot, and then the next one was even better. At 10 years old, I wondered if I could ever be like that."

Halfway around the globe, 16-year-old Ernie Els broke his curfew so he could stay up and watch the tournament with his father. There was a time difference of seven hours between Augusta and South Africa. "That was a special treat," Els told *Golfweek*. The leaderboard contained almost all of his favorites, the notable exception being fellow South African Gary Player, who had missed the thirty-six-hole cut. "I mean, if you look at that leaderboard, everybody that was anybody was on the leaderboard," Els said.

While weekend warriors and aspiring professionals looked on, Nicklaus had only five holes to go. The normally reserved Augusta crowd was buzzing as Nicklaus continued to climb up the leaderboard. He also had the biggest gallery following him, and it was difficult to get a close view as fans packed the areas around the greens and tees to better see him.

The 14th hole is the only one at Augusta National without a bunker, but the hole poses plenty of problems with its severely sloped green and false front.

After a perfect drive, Nicklaus had 155 yards to the flag, which was perched on a crest on the right side of the green. Only a perfectly executed shot would wind up close. Nicklaus took the long route and his ball wound up on the back fringe.

Nicklaus played his third shot expertly, and the ball took the slope and trickled down to tap-in range. The par kept him at 5-under with four to play.

Back at the 13th, Ballesteros hit a huge drive. His approach was the best of the day, and the ball hit the front of the green and bounced forward, catching the slope that runs through the middle of the green. It nestled to about 6 feet from the hole.

"I think he likes it," CBS's Ken Venturi said as Ballesteros smiled and took his visor off to acknowledge the patrons.

Kite, who had saved par with a lengthy putt at the 12th, also hit the 13th green in two. About the same distance as Nicklaus, Kite two-putted for his birdie and moved to 7-under.

Ballesteros knocked in his putt for eagle, his second of the day, and jumped to 9-under and two shots clear of Kite. The Spaniard's bid for a third green jacket was in good shape, and it appeared everyone else would battle for runner-up. He was the man to beat.

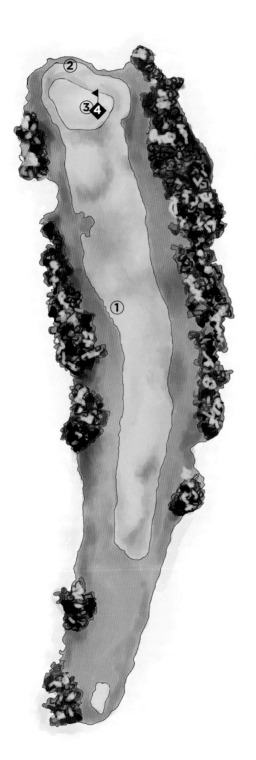

**Final Round
Jack Nicklaus on the 14th Hole**

Par 4, 405 yards

(1) 3-wood to right center of fairway
(2) 6-iron to back fringe
(3) and (4) Chip to 1 foot, made par

"I don't know that he was going to run away, but he was in pretty darn good shape," Nicklaus said.

Norman and Price were in the day's final pairing, but you couldn't tell it by their gallery size. The crowds had abandoned them as they sought out the action ahead of them. "I don't know what happened that day, if either of us were waiting for something to happen," Price said. "We both played fairly wishy-washy until 13 when we got fired up. We were standing back on the tee and not saying much to each other."

So the two challenged each other. "Jack had not started his run, he was playing well. Seve was playing well, Kite was playing well. We looked back and there were about 200 people there. Normally the whole gallery turns that fairway," Price said. "I said, 'Come on Greg, we've got to make something happen, man.' And that's what happened. We had two par-5s, two potential eagle holes, a few birdie holes."

Norman told a similar tale. "We both hit good shots into 14, and there were about 22 people behind the green," Norman said. "I said to Nicky that we need to show these people we're not out of the tournament. And we both made birdies and I put myself back into the competition."

CHAPTER 15

Hunting an Eagle

Augusta National's founding fathers, Bobby Jones and Clifford Roberts, made a wise decision when they reversed the nines before the 1935 Masters.

The first Masters in 1934 had been played with the nines opposite of how they are played today. A realization that the water holes would provide more drama, and a problem with the low-lying Amen Corner holes and morning frost, factored into their decision.

The move paid immediate dividends when Gene Sarazen holed his second shot at the 15th in the final round in 1935. The double eagle, the rarest shot in golf, enabled Sarazen to make up three shots on Craig Wood, and the next day he beat Wood in the tournament's only thirty-six-hole playoff.

Through the years, much drama and heartbreak has been recorded on the inward nine. The par-5 holes offer chances for eagles and easy birdies, but they also can punish errant shots with bogeys and double bogeys.

Historically the easiest hole on the course, the 15th was a 500-yard par-5 with a pond guarding the green. A well-struck drive could catch the downhill slope and leave a player with a shot of roughly 200 yards to the green.

By the time Nicklaus arrived at the hole Sunday, the 15th had given up three eagles on the day. The oddity was that all had occurred in the two groups preceding Nicklaus. First came Mark McCumber and Corey Pavin. McCumber's eagle put him at 5-under for the tournament, and Pavin's 3 was his second on the hole for the weekend. He vaulted to 6-under and into contention.

Gary Koch, playing alongside Bob Tway, followed up those eagles with one of his own. He moved to 2-under, but was too far back with three holes to go.

Nicklaus hit a perfect drive, and he was left with a shot of just over 200 yards. "I hit a big drive at 15, and I turned to Jackie and said, 'How far do you think a 3 will go here?'" Nicklaus said.

Jack Nicklaus eyes a putt during the final round of the 1986 Masters. Nicklaus played his final ten holes in 7-under par, and he matched the record (at the time) for the second nine with his score of 30.

Initially, Jackie thought he was talking about club selection. "I said that's the wrong club," Jackie said. "He said, 'I'm talking about an eagle.'"

Jackie quickly collected himself and said, "Let's see it."

Nicklaus's 4-iron was high and true, and it landed near the cup and settled about 12 feet away. "He's got a chance [for eagle]," Ben Wright said on the air. "The old bear is back."

As he made the walk toward the green, Nicklaus was greeted with another huge ovation.

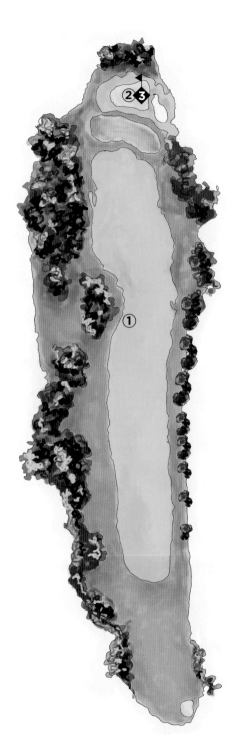

**Final Round
Jack Nicklaus on the 15th Hole**

Par 5, 500 yards

    (1) Driver to center of fairway
    (2) 4-iron to green
    (3) 12-foot putt for eagle

Up ahead, disaster had struck for Pavin. For the second day in a row, Pavin had followed up an eagle at 15 by hitting it in the water at 16 and making a double bogey. His chances were over.

Nicklaus backed off his eagle putt as applause from the Tway-Koch pairing at 16 made its way back to him. Settling into his familiar stance, Nicklaus sent the ball toward the hole. Jackie crouched down, then jumped into the air as the putt fell in and the gallery exploded in applause. "Yes sir!" Wright exclaimed.

Nicklaus wasn't sure how far behind he was, but he knew he was gaining ground. "I wasn't doing a whole lot of math about that time," he said. "I was too busy making birdies."

"That's when you started thinking, 'Wow,'" Jackie said. "I was very emotional, and trying not to look at him."

Jackie had caddied for his father at the 1982 U.S. Open at Pebble Beach, and on the final day the elder Nicklaus birdied five holes in a row to jump into contention. Jackie got caught up in the excitement, and at the eighth hole he became more of a cheerleader than caddie. Nicklaus bogeyed the hole, and eventually lost to Watson when he holed his famous chip at the 17th.

"I blamed myself for getting into his head emotionally, breaking his concentration," Jackie said.

After the eagle, Jackie struggled to control his emotions. Right after his jump for joy, he gathered himself.

"I remember taking that to 1986 when he was on his run," Jackie said. "There was no way I was going to let him see my excitement."

Up at the 18th hole, Rhett Sinclair put up a red 7 on the leaderboard for Nicklaus. "When he made that eagle they could hear the roar but you're sitting in front of 18 and you're thinking wow," Sinclair said. "When I opened the door to put that red number that was two numbers greater than the previous one, they started going crazy."

Nicklaus was now 7-under and tied with Kite, who had a short birdie putt at the 14th. But he missed it by leaving it short. Ballesteros, meanwhile, had made par at the 14th and was still two shots in front.

"Magnificent stuff," Wright said. "And that information will percolate back to Seve Ballesteros as he goes to the 15th tee."

Out of Hibernation

Jim Nantz is known by millions today as one of the country's leading broadcasters. He serves as anchor of the Masters broadcast and is CBS's lead play-by-play man for the NFL and NCAA men's basketball tournament games. But in 1986 Nantz was a Masters rookie, and he was assigned to the 16th hole.

Nantz had played on the college golf team at the University of Houston, where he had been a teammate of Fred Couples. But he knew his destiny was to announce the game, not play as a professional, and he would often entertain his teammates with calls of them winning the Masters. Now, Nantz had the spotlight to himself as he called the action as Nicklaus arrived on the 16th tee.

CBS first cut to the 15th tee, where Ballesteros hit a big drive. "That is huge, that is huge," Ben Wright said. "That is less than 200 yards from the green, I would say."

Kite also hit a perfect drive, and then the cameras cut back to Nicklaus as he prepared to play his tee shot. "Jack Nicklaus, knowing he must continue the charge," Nantz said. "He has to figure that Ballesteros will make at least a birdie back on 15. If anyone has ever owned this hole, it would be Jack Nicklaus."

Nantz recounted Nicklaus's birdie on the 16th in 1963 that gave him his first green jacket, and he told how Nicklaus had knocked in a 40-foot birdie putt in 1975 to beat Tom Weiskopf and Johnny Miller.

Weiskopf had never won the Masters—he was a four-time runner-up, including twice to Nicklaus—and he was now part of the CBS broadcast team. "Tom Weiskopf, what is going through Jack's mind right now?" Nantz asked. "He has not experienced this kind of a streak in a long time."

Weiskopf didn't miss a beat. "If I knew the way he thought, I would have won this tournament, Jim," Weiskopf replied. "No, seriously, he is going to

Final Round
Jack Nicklaus on the 16th Hole

Par 3, 170 yards

(1) 5-iron to green
(2) 3-foot birdie putt

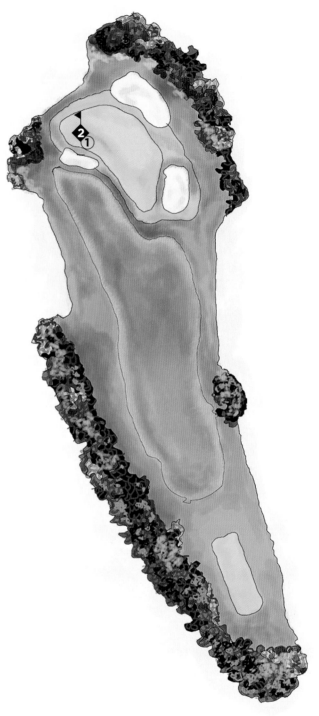

fire this right at the pin. He is going to think Jack, this is time right now, make the swing you are capable of making. Stay down, accelerate through the ball, make a good golf swing. Your destiny is right here."

Weiskopf's analysis was on the mark. Nicklaus fired his 5-iron at the pin, and he bent down to pick up his tee.

"Be right," Jackie said.

"It is," Nicklaus replied.

"He has such great belief in what he is doing. He knew it was the right club," Jackie said. "He doesn't say stuff like that. It was kind of an internally cocky comment. My reaction was wow, he's really dialed in."

The ball hit right of the pin, took the slope and nearly went into the cup for a hole-in-one. The gallery erupted.

"Oh my," Nantz said. "Back on the tee he clearly has no idea just how close he is." Nicklaus didn't see the ball land or where it wound up, but his ears were just fine.

"I've had a lot of great receptions at 16 in my life, but that one was pretty special," Nicklaus said. "I'm sure Ballesteros could have heard that if he was still back on the first tee."

He was left with 3 feet for birdie, and he described it as a "tricky left to right putt."

As Nicklaus walked the 170 yards to the green to a thunderous standing ovation, his play was clearly causing ripples all over the course. Tom Watson, putting for an eagle at the 15th, rushed his putt and missed. After surveying the putt, Nicklaus rolled in the birdie and the patrons roared their approval once again.

Nicklaus was now one stroke behind with two to play, and as Nicklaus retrieved his ball from the cup and headed for the 17th tee, Nantz said, "There is no doubt about it. The bear has come out of hibernation."

CHAPTER 17

Making Some Noise

Noise has an effect at the Masters unlike any other tournament in golf.

Longtime patrons and veteran journalists can identify a roar or loud ovation and pinpoint its location with frightening accuracy. Furthermore, they can tell you if it was for an eagle or a birdie, and they can also make an educated guess on which player it was for.

But this Sunday was different. The roars were larger than ever, and they rattled through the pines and rolled over the hills in rapid succession.

Nicklaus was the chief culprit, and as he prepared to tee off on the 17th a funny noise reached his ears. It came from the vicinity of the nearby 15th green, and it caused him to back off his shot. It was for Ballesteros's second shot, and it was not a good one. He had badly pulled his approach, and his ball splashed down into the middle of the pond.

Masters patrons consider themselves to be the most courteous in the game, but decorum went out the window, either because of shock or disbelief, or simply because so many were just rooting for Nicklaus. The gallery's response sent a message through the pines.

Nicklaus didn't care for that reaction from the gallery. "I heard that horrible sound, I knew exactly what it was, that sort of half cheer, half groan. The people that wanted me to win were cheering, and the people that wanted Seve to win were groaning," he said.

Ballesteros was obviously rattled by the reaction. "The whole thing if they cheered or not . . . of course they cheered," said Ron Green Jr., who covered it for the *Greenville News*. "All you have to do is watch the video."

Nicklaus regained his composure and struck his tee shot. His ball flew over Ike's Tree that guards the left side of the fairway, and hooked into the trees bordering the seventh green and 17th fairway.

Seve Ballesteros and rules officials discuss where he should take his penalty drop on the 15th hole after he hit it in the water on his second shot. Ballesteros held the lead entering the hole, but surrendered it when he hit into the pond in front of the green and made bogey.

Back at 15, Ballesteros took his drop and knocked his fourth shot onto the back of the green. His par putt missed, and now he was at 8-under along with Nicklaus.

Verne Lundquist was calling the action for CBS at the 17th, and it was his first year at that location. "And the Old Bear is oblivious to what has just happened at 15," Lundquist said as Nicklaus prepared to play his second shot from a tight lie between two pines from 110 yards away.

Nicklaus selected a pitching wedge, and he hit it low and with enough spin to grab and bite the green. The ball settled 11 feet from the pin, and now he had a chance to take the outright lead.

On the 17th green, Gary Koch and Bob Tway had watched Nicklaus hook his tee shot left of the fairway. They then finished the hole and waited to see what would unfold behind them. "You could kind of see back through there him hitting by the scoreboard and he runs that thing up there," Tway said. "People don't understand how great a shot that was to get there."

Meanwhile, Kite had hit the 15th green in two, and he had a putt for eagle. "I was trying to win a golf tournament and I wasn't paying much attention to what he was doing," Kite said of Ballesteros. "I had hit a beautiful 3-iron in there about 18 feet below the hole, and I was thinking about making my eagle."

He missed the eagle putt but tapped in for birdie to forge a three-way tie. And back at 14, fifty-four-hole leader Greg Norman had made three pars in a row after suffering the double bogey at 10. He got one shot back at the 14th though, when he rolled in a short birdie putt that put him at 6-under and two behind the tri-leaders.

At 17, the tension was high on the ground and in the broadcast booth as Nicklaus and his son discussed which way the putt would break.

Lundquist had only worked with the CBS golf crew for a few years, but veteran director Frank Chirkinian knew how to set up the drama. "We knew when Jack was getting ready that if he could do something magical on 17 he was going to be in good shape," Lundquist recalled. "We went elsewhere in the telecast, and I remember thinking, don't get in the way of this. Obviously you're aware he's looking at a birdie putt for the lead."

Nicklaus was facing an 11-footer, and again he and Jackie disagreed on the line. "Dad, it's got to go right," Nicklaus said his son told him. "I said, 'I know it's going to go right, Jack,' but I said, 'I think it's going to come back left at the hole.'" Years of experience told Nicklaus that Rae's Creek would hold the putt on a fairly straight line.

Sandy Lyle, Nicklaus's playing partner, said it was a "very, very, very hard putt to read."

"I don't think you can explain in words how difficult that was. He himself could barely read the green it was so crispy and fast," Lyle said. "It could go either way, you could knock it 6 foot past and miss a chance to be in a playoff or something like that."

It was a pivotal putt, and his fellow players recognized the moment. In the 15th fairway, Norman and Price were making their way down the hole. They had a clear view of Nicklaus on the green, which was ringed by fans. "We were walking down 15, walking past 17 green, which was to the right of us," Price said. "Jack was putting and so Greg and I slowed down so you can visually see through. We were just back and short of the green on the right."

In the broadcast booth, Lundquist waited patiently. "Frank [Chirkinian] took his time at getting to the shot, but he set it up," Lundquist said. "He gave me plenty of time."

As Nicklaus crouched into his stance, all was quiet. A train whistle could be heard in the background, the only audible noise. Then, Lundquist said, "This is for sole possession of the lead."

Nicklaus pulled back the Response ZT, and sent the ball on its way. With the ball a couple of feet from the hole, Nicklaus pursed his lips and raised his putter with his left hand. Lundquist pounced.

"Maybe . . . YES SIRRRR!"

Nicklaus raised both arms, breathed a sigh of relief and shook his head in disbelief. But it was true. A 46-year-old man had the lead in the final round of the Masters, and he only had one hole left to play.

"The ball went in, and I guess that was the first time I was leading in the tournament," Nicklaus said. "I didn't know that. All I knew was I was in pretty good shape."

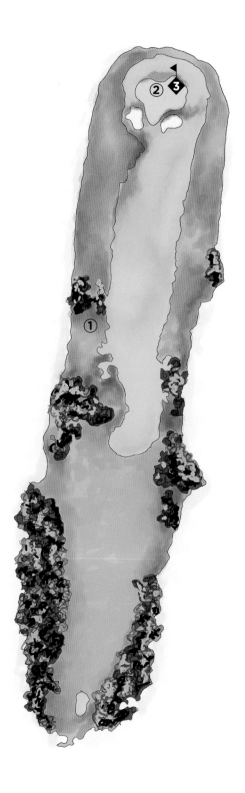

**Final Round
Jack Nicklaus on the 17th Hole**

Par 4, 400 yards

(1) Driver to left rough
(2) Pitching wedge to green
(3) 11-foot birdie putt

Nicklaus's reaction was priceless.

"All of a sudden he makes that putt at 17, and he's got that putter sticking out like a lance, and he's got that evil look on his face," Art Spander of the *San Francisco Chronicle* remembers.

Years later, Lundquist watched a VHS tape of the final round for the first time. "I just really, really enjoyed watching the telecast and reliving the experience," he said. "I said 'maybe,' then it dropped and the whole world exploded."

Some 300 yards ahead, at the 18th hole leaderboard, Rhett Sinclair was trembling as he prepared to post a red 9 for Nicklaus. "When he birdied 17, by that time I was wondering if I could stay up on that ladder and not fall down," he said.

After hitting his tee shot on the final hole, Tway had walked up the fairway and looked back. He couldn't see the green, but he heard the roar. Fans began running toward the 18th green. Tway turned to Koch and said, "Let's just get done."

The roars crashed through the pines. "We saw him hit the putt and saw him raise the putter and when the ball went in the hole, it was probably the loudest roar I've ever heard on a golf course," Price said. "It was deafening. People were running. It was frenzied. They were running to get spots on the next tee, to get up the next fairway. It was incredible."

CHAPTER 18

Coming Home

Jack Nicklaus went to the 18th tee at 9-under as the leader of the 50th Masters. It was the first time he had held sole possession of the lead in the final round in eleven years. It was a storyline almost too good to be true: the Golden Bear winning the golden anniversary of the Masters.

The putt at 17 sent golf writers who had been watching the drama unfold in the media center rushing to the 18th green. "There was a stampede," said Art Spander of the *San Francisco Chronicle*. "The Quonset hut was right off the [first fairway], and you could get out to the green a lot quicker then."

Ron Green Jr. had to come in from watching Nicklaus because he had to catch up with Jay Haas, but there was no way he was going to miss this moment. "I can't sit in there when this is happening," Green remembers thinking. "I could see him on the green, feel it. It was a magical day, part of why Augusta is Augusta."

Still, there was plenty of golf to be played. Behind Nicklaus there were a handful of players with chances to catch him. Ballesteros and Kite each made par at 16 and remained one shot behind. Norman made his second birdie in a row at the 15th and was two behind. Price had also birdied the 14th and 15th and was three behind.

Nicklaus had always been the model of concentration on the golf course, but now he found himself getting emotional. He knew he needed to make no worse than a par on the closing hole if he wanted to slip into the green jacket for an unprecedented sixth time.

"I kept getting tears in my eyes," Nicklaus said. "I kept saying, 'Hey, let's hold that back. You've got some golf to play.'"

The CBS announcers weren't outright pulling for Nicklaus, but it wasn't hard to see where their sentiment was. "Seven under today, five times a champion," Pat Summerall said as Nicklaus prepared to hit his final tee shot.

"[He] got a good break on 17, but when you're good, the breaks fall your way," Venturi responded. "And if there's any doubt about the greatness of this man . . . I think it's just phenomenal. Almost sold him out after he made bogey at 12."

The 18th hole at Augusta National is no pushover. At 405 yards, it played uphill and a slight fade was the desired shape of the tee shot. Golfers teed off from a thin chute, and a pair of bunkers guarded the left side of the landing area. They were put there after Nicklaus dominated the course in 1965 and set the seventy-two-hole scoring record.

But Nicklaus handled the shot with ease. It started on the left and cut back into the middle of the fairway. "You couldn't walk it out there any better, Pat," Venturi said.

Nicklaus still had work left, though. He faced a second shot of about 180 yards, and he chose a 5-iron. Nicklaus summed up all of the concentration powers—the ones that had helped him win a record seventeen professional majors—and played the shot almost perfectly.

Nicklaus's shot was on line, but it hit on the bottom tier of the green and wound up 35–40 feet from the cup. "As soon as I hit it I felt the rush of wind in my face," Nicklaus said. "I said, 'It's not going to get there.'"

There isn't a better feeling in golf than to walk up the 18th fairway on Sunday with the lead at the Masters. Nicklaus's ears were ringing by the time he reached the green. "The ovation was unbelievable," he said. "I couldn't hear a thing."

On the leaderboard at 18, Rhett Sinclair was caught up in the moment.

"When he came up 18 and I'm standing on top of that ladder, they're on these tracks so they won't fall off. I slid all the way to the left closest to the fairway," Sinclair said. "As Nicklaus is coming up, I got chills. I was almost shaking and that's when I'm going yeah [and pumping his arm in celebration]."

He wasn't alone. The ovation lasted the duration of Nicklaus's walk to the green and continued as he surveyed his birdie putt.

Nicklaus needed to navigate the 40 feet in two putts. He turned off the emotion as best he could and concentrated on the task at hand.

Jack Nicklaus and his caddie and son, Jackie, walk up the 18th fairway in the final round. Nicklaus fought back tears on the final nine as he won his sixth and final green jacket.

Final Round
Jack Nicklaus on the 18th Hole

Par 4, 405 yards

(1) 3-wood to center of fairway
(2) 5-iron to green
(3) and (4) Two putts from 40 feet
for par

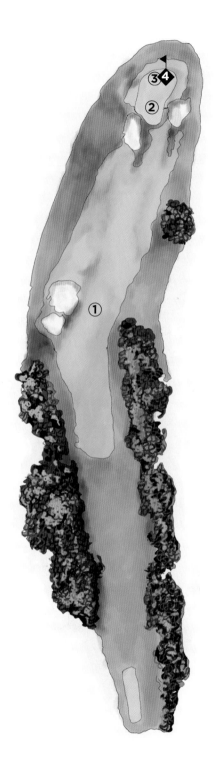

Nicklaus had an advantage on that putt that few realized. The 9th and 18th greens had been altered that year to lessen the severity of the slopes. Bob Cupp, who had worked for Nicklaus's course design company, was in charge of the work. Nicklaus had worked on the putt in his practice rounds.

"I said don't leave yourself a second putt," Nicklaus said, and he didn't. The putt chugged up the hill on a beeline for the hole, but lost steam and curled away at the very end.

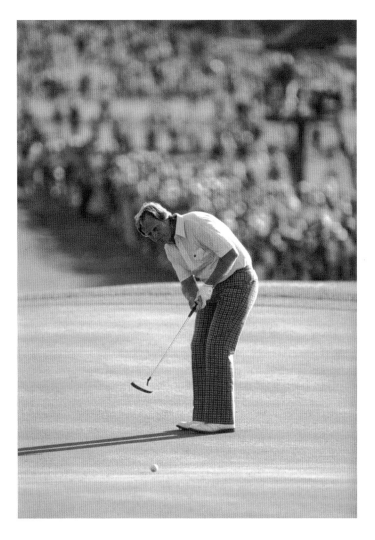

Jack Nicklaus watches as his birdie putt from 40 feet on the final hole of the 1986 Masters heads toward the hole. Nicklaus missed the putt, but tapped in for a par and a final-round 65.

Clay Long, the putter designer, said the most nervous he got was when Nicklaus stood over the long putt at 18. "If he three-putts from there that putter will be the goat of the earth," he said. "That is a horrifically difficult putt. But he put it in the leather."

Nicklaus tapped in for his par. His numbers were staggering: a 65 for the 18, a 30 on the final nine and 7-under for his final ten holes.

At 9-under, he held the clubhouse lead. Now, he had to see if anyone could match him.

After shaking hands with Sandy Lyle and his caddie, Nicklaus turned to his son. The two embraced, and walked off the green with their arms around each other.

After Nicklaus signed his scorecard, he was whisked away to Jones Cabin. There, he and his son would wait and see if anyone could catch him.

"We both knew he had done all he could do," Jackie said.

Back at 17, Ballesteros had pulled his second shot and was left with a long, tricky putt. After backing off because of the Nicklaus ovations, Ballesteros's birdie putt ran well past the hole. He missed the comebacker, and his chances for a third Masters title were over. The gallery, realizing the situation, gave Ballesteros a warm ovation. The Spaniard said "thank you" and tipped his cap.

Kite had a birdie putt, but he missed and would need to birdie the 18th hole to force a tie.

OFFICIAL SCORECARD — Sunday April 13, 1986

Hole	1	2	3	4	5	6	7	8	9	Out	10	11	12	13	14	15	16	17	18	In	Totals
Yardage	400	555	360	205	435	180	360	535	435	3465	485	455	155	465	405	500	170	400	405	3440	6905
Par	4	5	4	3	4	3	4	5	4	36	4	4	3	5	4	5	3	4	4	36	72
Player	4	4	4	4	4	3	4	5	3	35	3	3	4	4	4	3	2	3	4	30	65

ATTEST _____

I HAVE CHECKED MY SCORE HOLE BY HOLE.
PLAYER SIGNATURE _____ Jack Nicklaus

Jack Nicklaus's scorecard for the final round of the 1986 Masters Tournament featured one eagle, seven birdies, eight pars, and two bogeys. The 7-under-par 65 was the lowest final round for Nicklaus in his forty-five Masters appearances.

Seve Ballesteros acknowledges fans late in the final round of the 1986 Masters. Ballesteros three-putted the 17th hole to lose any hope of catching Jack Nicklaus.

And back at the 16th, Norman duplicated Nicklaus's tee shot. He made birdie, his third in a row, to pull one behind.

"I walked off the green knowing that I'd put myself in a position to win the golf tournament," Nicklaus said.

Only two men could catch Nicklaus now. The Golden Bear, in the twilight of his career, had done everything he could. Now, it was out of his hands.

CHAPTER 19

The Remaining Challengers

The first challenger was Tom Kite, who was one behind with one to play. Kite had never won a major, but he was one of the top players on the PGA Tour. He had his best chance at Augusta back in 1984 when he held the fifty-four-hole lead, but longtime rival Ben Crenshaw overcame him to win his first Masters. Kite shot 75, including a triple bogey on the 12th when he found the water, and finished tied for sixth.

Kite finished second to Ballesteros in 1983, but he was four shots behind and never in serious contention. Now, he was battling the best in the world and the man many considered the best to ever play the game.

"Didn't look like Jack was in the tournament," Kite said. "It was between Norman and Seve and myself, and I think everyone anticipated one of the three of us winning."

After a perfect drive at the 18th, Kite was left with 165 yards. His 6-iron caught the top of the slope and bounced toward the pin, settling about 10 feet away.

Kite settled over the putt, and when it left his putter he felt he had made it. But it lost its speed and dived left at the very end. Kite, who had practiced that putt multiple times, couldn't believe it. "I hit a good putt. It just hung out on the right side," he said. "Had a great chance to go in. Wish it would have."

The Nicklauses could breathe a sign of relief. "Kite hit a really nice second shot in there and a really nice putt," Nicklaus said. "It didn't have quite the speed to carry through on the putt."

That left Greg Norman as the last man standing between Nicklaus and an unprecedented eighteenth professional major championship.

Like Kite, Norman was still looking for his first major title. He had made a splash at his first Masters in 1981, and he had lost an eighteen-hole playoff to Fuzzy Zoeller at the 1984 U.S. Open at Winged Foot.

(Left) Tom Kite hangs his head in disbelief after missing his birdie putt at the final hole of the 1986 Masters. A birdie would have put Kite into a tie with Jack Nicklaus and forced a sudden-death playoff.

(Below) Tom Kite acknowledges the gallery during the final round of the 1986 Masters. Kite would finish tied for second at the Masters three times in his career.

Through the years, many players had been burdened by the label of being "the next Nicklaus," but Norman seemed like a worthy candidate. With his powerful game, many felt he was a safe bet to win multiple Masters titles before his career was through.

After making the double bogey at 10, Norman settled down and played solid golf. He parred the next three holes, then got on a roll with birdies at the 14th, 15th, and 16th.

The gallery, which had been so sparse only a few holes before, began to return.

"All of a sudden the whole crowd is coming down the mountain," Norman said. "It was amazing to see the movement of the gallery."

As he headed to the 17th, Norman was only one behind Nicklaus. But his tee shot wound up in a precarious spot, well left of the fairway and short of the adjoining 7th green. His ball wound up in a sprinkler head, and he received a free drop.

That was the least of his problems. To get to the green, he would have to hit through and underneath the pine trees in front of him. Norman pulled off an incredible shot, a low runner that hit short of the 17th green and bounced onto the putting surface. The ball settled some 12 feet from the hole.

"That second shot was one of the best shots I've ever seen in my life under major championship pressure," playing partner Nick Price said. "It was frighteningly good."

Norman said it was all "visualization and confidence. I had a shot and took it. There was no chance of me laying up and trying to make four."

Verne Lundquist again had the call. "One challenger left, and the name is Norman," Lundquist said. "He's got that much left to tie Nicklaus."

Norman poured the putt into the middle of the cup, his fourth birdie in a row, and he was tied with Nicklaus. "Yes sir!" Lundquist exclaimed.

Now there was a two-way tie, and all eyes turned to Norman as he played the 18th.

Back in the Jones Cabin, Nicklaus and son could only watch. "That was the hardest part. My stomach was in knots," Jackie said. "My dad and I are sitting there, and he got up and started walking around. That was the toughest part."

A sudden-death playoff seemed likely. While many patrons headed for the 18th green, to see a possible birdie by Norman, others headed for 10 and 11. The Masters had used eighteen-hole playoffs to settle ties after Gene Sarazen and Craig Wood's epic thirty-six-hole playoff in 1935. The tournament, though, announced in 1976 that it would go to the more TV-friendly format of sudden death. Play would begin on 10 and would keep going as long as necessary. The first sudden-death playoff came in 1979, and Fuzzy Zoeller sank a birdie putt at the 11th to defeat Tom Watson and Ed Sneed. Three years later, Craig Stadler only needed one hole to beat Dan Pohl.

Norman's 3-wood tee shot was perfect. It split the fairway and left him about 185 yards to the pin. He selected a 4-iron for the shot up the hill. But the ball sailed right, into the gallery, and Norman hung his head in disbelief.

"I was basically trying to go for the three as well as playing for the four," Norman told reporters after the round. "It was a shot I was trying to play for, but I just didn't make a good swing at."

Price couldn't believe what he just saw. "He played unbelievable those last six holes until he got to the 18th hole and hit one of the worst second shots I've ever seen him hit," Price said.

His friend also said he would have gone with a different club. "If I'd been his caddie that day, 4-iron was the club to fly the ball back to the hole. I

Greg Norman prepares to play his third shot at the final hole of the 1986 Masters. Norman's second shot sailed into the gallery right of the green, leaving him this difficult shot. He knocked it on the green but missed the par putt, dropping him into a tie for second place.

think I would have been more prone to give him the 5-iron," Price said. "And see if he could have hit a hard one and run it up that slope. And if it got down to the bottom of that slope, see if he can make a 30-footer to win. But he was playing to win. He was so fired up. It was wonderful to watch."

Now Norman faced the daunting task of getting up and down for par to force a playoff with Nicklaus. After the gallery was cleared, Norman settled over his shot. It wasn't an ideal lie.

"On the chip shot, the ball was sitting firm because the gallery had packed the grass down," Norman said. "I only had one option—to play bump and run and try to let the ball trickle off the top tier of the green."

The low, running chip hit the green and chased past the cup. He had 16 feet left to force a playoff. A superstitious Nicklaus was watching it all unfold on TV, even though the live action was about 100 yards away.

"I was sitting on the couch watching them and Norman kept making birdies. I said I'm not doing very well here," Nicklaus said. "So I got up and

Greg Norman studies his putt for par on the final hole. Norman missed it and finished tied for second with Tom Kite.

walked around the room and stood behind the couch. Then he played 18. I wasn't wishing anybody bad luck. The guy kept making birdies and I was sitting there watching him."

Norman's putt never scared the hole. His bogey dropped him back to 8-under, and the impossible had happened.

Jack Nicklaus, at age 46, thought to be too old and washed up, had won the Masters for a sixth time. In the Jones Cabin, father and son embraced again.

"I gave him a hug," Jackie said. "It was great."

LEADERBOARD

FOURTH ROUND

SUNDAY, APRIL 13

POSITION	PLAYER	ROUND ONE	ROUND TWO	ROUND THREE	ROUND FOUR	TOTAL STROKES
1	JACK NICKLAUS	74	71	69	65	279
T2	TOM KITE	70	74	68	68	280
T2	GREG NORMAN	70	72	68	70	280
4	SEVE BALLESTEROS	71	68	72	70	281
5	NICK PRICE	79	69	63	71	282
T6	JAY HAAS	76	69	71	67	283
T6	TOM WATSON	70	74	68	71	283
T8	TOMMY NAKAJIMA	70	71	71	72	284
T8	PAYNE STEWART	75	71	69	69	284
T8	BOB TWAY	70	73	71	70	284
T11	DONNIE HAMMOND	73	71	67	74	285
T11	SANDY LYLE	76	70	68	71	285
T11	MARK MCCUMBER	76	67	71	71	285
T11	COREY PAVIN	71	72	71	71	285
T11	CALVIN PEETE	75	71	69	70	285

T16	DAVE BARR	70	77	71	68	286
T16	BEN CRENSHAW	71	71	74	70	286
T16	GARY KOCH	69	74	71	72	286
T16	BERNHARD LANGER	74	68	69	75	286
T16	LARRY MIZE	75	74	72	65	286
T21	CURTIS STRANGE	73	74	68	72	287
T21	FUZZY ZOELLER	73	73	69	72	287
T23	T.C. CHEN	69	73	75	71	288
T23	ROGER MALTBIE	71	75	69	73	288
T25	BILL GLASSON	72	74	72	71	289
T25	PETER JACOBSEN	75	73	68	73	289
T25	SCOTT SIMPSON	76	72	67	74	289
T28	DANNY EDWARDS	71	71	72	76	290
T28	DAVID GRAHAM	76	72	74	68	290
T28	JOHNNY MILLER	74	70	77	69	290
T31	FRED COUPLES	72	77	70	72	291
T31	BRUCE LIETZKE	78	70	68	75	291
T31	DAN POHL	76	70	72	73	291
T31	LANNY WADKINS	78	71	73	69	291
35	WAYNE LEVI	73	76	67	76	292
T36	RICK FEHR	75	74	69	75	293
T36	HUBERT GREEN	71	75	73	74	293
T36	LARRY NELSON	73	73	71	76	293
T36	ASAM RANDOLPH	75	73	72	73	293
T36	TONY SILLS	76	73	73	71	293
41	DON POOLEY	77	72	73	72	294
T42	BILL KRATZERT	68	72	76	79	295
T42	JOHN MAHAFFEY	79	69	72	75	295
44	KEN GREEN	68	78	74	76	296
T45	PHIL BLACKMAR	76	73	73	76	298
T45	JIM THORPE	74	74	73	77	298
47	LEE TREVINO	76	73	73	77	299
48	MARK O'MEARA	74	73	81	73	301

CHAPTER 20

Sunday Night

A phalanx of Pinkerton guards escorted Nicklaus the short distance from Jones Cabin to Butler Cabin, where the winner would be presented his green jacket in the live TV ceremony.

"It was really cute because when the last putt was in and it was sure he was the winner, the policemen who came to the door to take him out there were so ecstatic," Barbara Nicklaus said. "Everyone was so happy for Jack. It was fantastic."

Fans swarmed the area as a grinning Nicklaus made his way down the steps into the Butler Cabin. There, defending champion Bernhard Langer and chairman Hord Hardin waited for him.

Everyone was in a state of disbelief. Nick Price found Sandy Lyle in the locker room afterward. "I said to Sandy, 'What was that like?' He went, 'Oh my God,'" Price said. "He rolled his eyes and said I've never seen anything like it or felt anything like it."

As the patrons gathered for the green jacket ceremony held on the practice putting green, David Westin of the *Augusta Chronicle* caught up with a proud wife and proud son. "It was great, they really get along so well," Barbara Nicklaus said. "They have such a good time together and they're so relaxed together that it was really nice."

The younger Nicklaus had also been the caddie for his father's last win, the 1984 Memorial Tournament. That tournament was founded by Nicklaus in 1976 and held on his course, Muirfield Village, in Dublin, Ohio.

"He asked me to caddie for him about a month or month and a half ago and I jumped at it," Jackie said. "Willie Peterson caddied for over twenty years for my dad here but he wanted to try something different a couple of years ago and he had some of his tour caddies come over. He let me caddie for him this week."

According to the son, the father knew it was time for him to kickstart his season. "I remember we were walking on the fifth fairway and he said, 'I've made $4,000 coming into this tournament, which is an off season for me, but the season begins right now,'" Jackie said.

After three days of not getting any putts to drop, Jackie said his father was patient. "He just had to get some confidence. He was patient and then all of a sudden he really got some confidence and that was the whole difference," Jackie said. "He started rolling in putts."

The Masters victory was worth $144,000 for Nicklaus, the biggest check he would ever earn at Augusta, and more than his five previous Masters wins combined ($125,000). But it was priceless for what it meant to him in the twilight of his career.

Bernhard Langer helps Jack Nicklaus slip into his green jacket in 1986. Custom calls for the defending champion to help the winner into his garment.

Jack Nicklaus speaks at the green jacket ceremony following his victory.

As the sun began to set over Augusta National, emotion finally overtook Nicklaus as he addressed the patrons who had gathered to see him slip into his sixth green jacket.

And why not? His mother, sister, wife, and son were all on hand for his most memorable, and unexpected, triumph.

After brief speeches, Bernhard Langer helped Nicklaus put on the green garment. The jacket is the ultimate symbol of success in golf, and Nicklaus was donning it for a sixth time.

"I kept getting tears in my eyes," Nicklaus said at the ceremony as he compared it to his victories at St. Andrews in 1978 and the U.S. Open in 1980. "Coming down the stretch was an experience I won't soon forget."

While Nicklaus went through the ceremonies, the others made their way through interviews. Norman said he was proud of the way he hung in the tournament after making a double bogey at the 10th.

"I know I gave 101 percent and never gave up. What do you want me to do, cry?" Norman said. "I knew I needed four or five birdies on the finishing holes to win. I gave it my best shot. That's all I can do."

The Australian didn't downplay the significance of Nicklaus's win. "Jack's special and I know this was special for him. Maybe next year will be my year," he said. "It's OK, because I know one of these days, I'm gonna break his record of six Masters anyway."

Kite was still wondering how his birdie putt at the final hole missed. But he still gave credit to Nicklaus. "Two years ago, I feel like I lost that tournament. This tournament, Jack won," Kite said. "I knew it was in [his putt at 18]. I made that putt. How it did what it did, I'll never know."

Ballesteros didn't come to the interview area, but Thomas Stinson of the *Atlanta Constitution* caught up with the Spaniard before he could leave the grounds. Ballesteros had brashly predicted earlier in the week that the tournament would be over by the 16th hole Sunday, and for him, it was. His second shot into the pond at 15 effectively knocked him out of the running.

According to Stinson's story, Ballesteros was unsure of what club to hit. He and his brother/caddie finally settled on the 4-iron. "Hard to know what happened. I wasn't nervous," Ballesteros said. "I think I tried to hit a 4-iron too easy. I should have hit a 5-iron. It's the only bad swing I had all day. It cost me the tournament, maybe."

Ballesteros took a moment to give Nicklaus credit. And maybe a little jab, too.

"Nicklaus played well and he deserved to win," Ballesteros said. "It's nice to see an American win the Masters again."

CHAPTER 21

Media Coverage

Over in the Quonset hut, the area that served as the press center, bedlam ensued as writers on deadline worked feverishly to file their stories. Others tried to start writing before Nicklaus made his way there for the customary winner's interview.

Ward Clayton, the Durham, North Carolina, golf writer who would later become sports editor of the *Augusta Chronicle*, recalls the scene. "At tournament's end, it was like the media center had become a big cheering section, not just to root on Nicklaus but because the story was so unbelievable," Clayton said. "The best lead that was written was by a writer I cannot remember: 'My fingers will not work.'"

It was Rick Reilly's first Masters, and the *Sports Illustrated* writer remembers his fellow journalists being in awe. "Seeing guys trying to write afterwards, I remember one old guy clutching his hair and saying, 'It's too big, it's too big.'"

Reilly had been at the 18th green when Nicklaus finished, and one scene struck him.

It wasn't the father-son embrace. Rather, it was the scorekeeper who had posted the final numbers for Nicklaus and Norman, and he was pumping his arm in celebration.

"We saw the number change from 8 to 9, and a guy put his arm up from behind and goes like this. And the place goes crazy," said Reilly, gesturing with his hand. "I wouldn't recognize him, but I would recognize his arm."

It was Rhett Sinclair, the University of South Carolina—Aiken golfer who was caught up in Nicklaus's win. So Reilly fell back on a piece of advice he had remembered from years before.

"I used the old Jimmy Breslin line. The bigger the moment the smaller you go," he said. "When he attended Kennedy's funeral he wrote about the guy digging his grave. The tweed coat, the tweed hat. That always stuck with me. I wanted to focus on something really small. So I got the guy's arm."

Reilly wrote in his cover story in the following week's *Sports Illustrated*: "No head, no body, no shoulder, just an arm belonging to the leaderboard man, pumping and pumping for pure, wallowing joy. To hell with employee objectivity, Jack Nicklaus had just won the Masters, once again, and that arm just couldn't help itself."

Hubert Mizell of the *St. Petersburg Times* said he remembers his mind racing as he tried to figure out "how am I going to tell this story."

"I remember thinking, 'This might be too big for me,'" Mizell said. "That's when I tried to take a more simple approach, of allowing the bare facts and human drama to carry me through the paragraphs."

Nicklaus finally arrived in the interview room, and the golf writers and columnists filled the room. According to Glenn Sheeley's article in the *Atlanta Journal*, Nicklaus began to describe his feelings about the win when he broke off in mid-sentence.

"Where's Tom McCollister?" Nicklaus asked.

"He's not here," someone replied.

"I didn't think he would be," Nicklaus said.

Actually, McCollister was on deadline and finishing up a story for the *Constitution*.

When he came in to the interview room a few minutes later, Nicklaus spotted him.

"Hi Tom . . . thanks," Nicklaus said.

McCollister didn't skip a beat. "Glad I could help," he replied.

According to Sheeley, McCollister's kicker line wasn't heard by many people.

"Under the laughter, Tom said, 'Watson wants me to write about him next year.' Only a few people heard it," Sheeley said. "I thought it was the funniest line."

Hard to believe, but just seven days earlier McCollister had penned these words: "Nicklaus is gone, done. He just doesn't have the game anymore. It's rusted from lack of use. He's 46, and nobody that old wins the Masters."

Nicklaus was no longer bothered by the words.

"You just write the same article next year, and put 47 years old in it," Nicklaus said with a smile.

"Not me," McCollister said. "I believe you."

While the writers scrambled to file their stories, Nicklaus and his family enjoyed the traditional champion's dinner with Augusta National members in the clubhouse. Then the Nicklaus group boarded his private jet and flew home to Florida.

Nicklaus was greeted Monday morning by sensational overnight reviews for his stirring victory.

In the *Augusta Chronicle*, where the winner always received front-page treatment, the Nicklaus win received a two-deck headline that stretched across the front page: JACK'S BACK, ROARS OUT OF PACK WITH 65 FOR SIXTH MASTERS TITLE. And the subhead: NICKLAUS SILENCES CRITICS WITH GRAND PERFORMANCE.

Roger Whiddon's lead in the *Chronicle* summed it up. "The king of golf is not ready to relinquish his crown. Jack Nicklaus, with a career unmatched in the sport, has been scorned by his subjects. His pride hurt, the questions kept coming. 'When will you step down, retire?' 'It said I was dead, washed up, through, with no chance whatsoever to win again. I was sizzling,' said Nicklaus. 'I kept thinking, 'Dead, huh? Washed up, huh?'"

From coast to coast, the writers gushed.

Dave Anderson wrote in the *New York Times*: "But Sunday, Jack Nicklaus reminded the world he was still Jack Nicklaus, the best golfer in history. He shot 65 and put on the Masters green jacket for the sixth time. He turned Augusta National into a theater in the pines. He heard the cheers. He felt the tears."

In the *Washington Post*, Thomas Boswell's front page story began: "Some things cannot possibly happen, because they are both too improbable and too perfect."

Bob Verdi, in the *Chicago Tribune*, wrote about the source of Nicklaus's inspiration. "Jack Nicklaus had been told too often lately that his putting stroke had gone soft and his arteries hard, that the sooner he took a graceful bow, the better. He had just read another obit recently, in fact."

In the *Los Angeles Times*, Mike Downey put the win in perspective: "He reminisces about spectators 'hanging from the rafters' at St. Andrews in Scotland, when he won the British Open in 1978. That was emotional for him. He remembers the gallery's roar at Baltusrol in 1980, when the U.S. Open was his. That was emotional. But never has a crowd been louder. Never a victory so popular. Never one that felt so right."

The *Atlanta Journal*'s Furman Bisher, who was a personal friend of Bobby Jones and who gave Byron Nelson his nickname "Lord Byron," compared it to some of the biggest feats in golf. "Was it the biggest thing in American golf since Ben Hogan's Pro Slam in 1953? Was it the biggest since Bobby Jones' Grand Slam in 1930? Was it only bigger than Arnold Palmer's first accredited charge in 1960, when he caught and passed Ken Venturi and set golf off on this rampant run to glory?" Bisher wrote. "Whatever the size of it, there hasn't been a sports event in years that sent so many Americans home from the game or away from the television set with such an afterglow."

The magazine writers had their say too.

Dan Jenkins, in the June issue of *Golf Digest*, wrote: "If you want to put golf back on the front pages again and you don't have a Bobby Jones or a Francis Ouimet handy, here's what you do: You send an aging Jack Nicklaus out in the last round of the Masters and let him kill more foreigners than a general named Eisenhower."

Nicklaus landed the *Sports Illustrated* cover the following week with the headline ONE FOR THE AGES. "It is a trick no other golf god has pulled, not Palmer or Hogan or Snead or Sarazen," Rick Reilly wrote. "Nicklaus had beaten young men at a young man's game on young men's greens and beaten them when they were at their youthful best."

The two men who helped inspire Nicklaus's victory—golf writer Tom McCollister and practical joker John Montgomery—got satisfaction out of their roles. Eight days after writing off Nicklaus, McCollister's piece in the *Atlanta Constitution* marveled at the skills of a 46-year-old man.

"His driving was vintage Nicklaus, awesomely long. His approach shots were crisp and on the stick," McCollister wrote. "His putting was deadly. Like a man possessed, seeking that one last hurrah, he made time stand still."

McCollister enjoyed his fifteen minutes of fame as he was interviewed on the fifth and tenth anniversaries of the 1986 tournament. "He began to appreciate the fact that he had been glorified," Bisher said.

His colleagues remember him as a good guy who never intended to hurt Nicklaus's feelings. "Tommy's a hell of a guy. He had a lot of friends," said Marino Parascenzo, the golf writer for the *Pittsburgh Post-Gazette*. "I wasn't aware he had written that until Jack brought it up and said he posted it on his refrigerator."

Sadly, McCollister was killed in an automobile accident about a month before the 1999 Masters. "It's just a shame. He had been out practicing on the driving range and somehow [his car] got tangled up in a traffic turn and some woman hit his car on the opposite side. It killed him," Bisher said. "He'd been off golf beat but he was being put back, and he never got to it. It was a shame."

"Tom McCollister was the kind of fellow that when you talked to him, you knew it was going to come out the way you said it," Nicklaus said in the obituary that appeared in the Atlanta newspaper. "I never had any trouble talking with Tom McCollister."

John Montgomery, who taped McCollister's article to the refrigerator, died in 2007. He was 80. His obituary said Montgomery "became a Master of Golf Tournament Operations throughout the world."

At a memorial service held at the TPC Sawgrass Clubhouse in Ponte Vedra, Florida, writer Tim Rosaforte reported that a who's who of the golf world showed up to pay their respects to Montgomery.

"A writer once said that there are three types of golf tournaments," PGA Tour commissioner Tim Finchem said. "Tournaments that aren't run by Montgomery. Tournaments that are run by Montgomery. And tournaments that want to be run by Montgomery."

Montgomery, though, will forever be linked to his role in the 1986 Masters.

"But if Montgomery was famous for anything, it was helping to write a page in golf history—and perhaps motivate Nicklaus to his greatest triumph," Rosaforte wrote in *Golf World*. "As Nicklaus said concluding the service, John's probably still laughing about that one. It was part of the legacy he left behind."

CHAPTER 22

The Putter Part II

Clay Long and the folks at MacGregor Golf could not have anticipated the response to the Response ZT Nicklaus used to win the Masters. "Monday morning before noon we got 5,000 phone-in orders," Long said. "We ended up before 1986 was over selling 125,000 putters, which is all we could make. The casting factory in California was full, and the Albany plant was full of aluminum putters."

There is not a comparable success story in golf with a player winning a major and the next day sales of a key club going through the roof. The only comparison Long could come up with is if 59-year-old Tom Watson had won the British Open in 2009, instead of losing in a playoff to Stewart Cink.

"If Tom Watson had won the British Open, if he'd shot 30 on the last nine holes at Turnberry and he'd been putting with the first two-ball putter ever made, that might have been a close second," Long said. "Here's a guy [Nicklaus] who's over the hill, too old, but he's going to win, and he's going to shoot 30. And he's using a putter that no one's ever seen."

Although the putter had sold well before the Masters, word was slow getting out about it. Remember, there was no Internet back then, no social media or proliferation of cable television channels.

"Our ad campaign for that putter, and back in those days MacGregor had no money to advertise, was $60,000 and we had thirteen weeks in *Golf World*," Long said. "It just so happened the first ad broke in *Golf World* in the Masters Edition. That was planned way back in January. You watch that on television and on Wednesday in my mailbox here's *Golf World* and a big picture of him with that putter. He had a good time with it. He had a ball winning it. We all felt like we were walking down the fairway with him at the time."

Jack Nicklaus rolls in a 25-foot birdie putt at the 10th hole in the final round of the 1986 Masters. Nicklaus was using the oversized MacGregor Response ZT putter for the first time in a major.

Long and MacGregor Golf parted ways before 1992. He became an independent designer and did work for Arnold Palmer before moving to Southern California in 1997 to become head of research and development for Cobra.

Long left Cobra in 2000, and he was contacted by Nicklaus's equipment company in early 2001. He became the chief designer for the Nicklaus line of clubs and remains in that position today. Long owns and operates Plus 2 International, which specializes in golf club design and product development.

"To this day, honestly, if I try to sit down and talk about it I get choked up about it," Long said. "It was so emotionally filled. What it meant to all of us who were involved at the company. It really kind of saved the company. We had a banner year that year and were profitable the next year. We sold all our products after that [Response ZT] got hot. The stars really lined up during that episode."

Long might not be a household name outside of golf's inner circle, but he will forever be associated with Nicklaus's final major win. "It was really a phenomenal thing. It's been twenty-five years, and that club's almost an antique," Long said. "When I play golf now, I play with a lot of people who were 3 when it happened. But a lot of people my age know exactly where they were when it happened. It's one of those things you don't forget. I'm lucky to have experienced that."

MacGregor Golf was not as fortunate as Long. Nicklaus sold the majority of his interest in the company in late 1986, and then sold the remaining portion in 1992 when he formed his own company. The company floundered for many years, and in 2006 Greg Norman bought into MacGregor.

But even the Great White Shark, who enjoyed many business successes, couldn't right this ship. He bailed out and now endorses TaylorMade clubs. In 2009, MacGregor was acquired by golf retailer Golfsmith International.

"It's a shame in many ways," Nicklaus said in a *Golfweek* article on the company's demise. "MacGregor was a name and a company that was at the head of the industry for forty or fifty years. Then things changed."

And whatever happened to the putter that Nicklaus used that fateful day in 1986?

Nicklaus doesn't have it, nor does he know where it is.

"Oddly enough, it's the only golf club that I won a major with that I don't have," Nicklaus said in 2006.

CHAPTER 23

Congratulations and Inspiration

Congratulations from all over the world poured in after the unexpected win. From fellow golfers to movie stars to politicians, the well-wishers had their say.

According to the Nicklaus website, the notables included the following:

A typed note from Arnold Palmer: "Jack, I think it was fantastic, congratulations. Arn. P.S. Do you think there's a chance for a 56 year old?"

A telegram from Lee Trevino: "Congratulations. Great last round. From your #1 fan."

A handwritten note from George H. W. Bush, vice president of the United States, with the notation "TV still on" in the corner: "Dear Jack— Great win! What a thrill for all your fans—that means me! Congratulations."

A telephone message from Sean Connery: "Really—it was wonderful. Look forward to seeing you soon."

A note from Byron Nelson: "You certainly played great. I am proud of you. The most exciting Masters of all time. My sincere congratulations to a great champion."

The Nicklaus win also had an unexpected effect: His victory inspired other "aging" athletes.

Barely three weeks after Nicklaus slipped on his sixth green jacket, a couple of other stars who were thought to be past their prime stepped up and shocked the sports world.

First was legendary jockey Bill Shoemaker, who was 54. On the first Saturday in May, at the Kentucky Derby, he guided Ferdinand from dead last to first place and a spot in the winner's circle. It was Shoemaker's fourth win at Churchill Downs and his first since he rode Lucky Debonair to the win in 1965.

Shoemaker, an avid golfer, said he drew inspiration from watching Nicklaus win in Augusta. He and his wife, Cindy, had watched the golf tournament at their home.

"This is the omen, Cindy. They thought he was washed up, finished, and he just won the Masters," Shoemaker said in *Sports Illustrated*. "If Nicklaus can win the Masters, I can win the Kentucky Derby."

The very next day, another "jockey" guided his entry to first place in a race. Only Bobby Allison, 48, was in the driver's seat of a Buick LeSabre, and his victory came in the Winston 500 at Talladega, Alabama.

The win was the eighty-second of Allison's career but the first in two years, a span of fifty-five races. It also made him the oldest man to win a NASCAR race. (Allison's last win had come on May 27, 1984, which happened to be the same day that Nicklaus had won the Memorial Tournament for his last victory prior to the Masters.)

The Talladega race was billed as the fastest in stock car history as the forty qualifiers averaged 205.339 mph around the oval. Bill Elliott set an all-time qualifying record with a lap of 212.229 mph.

Elliott, however, bowed out late in the race when his transmission gave way. That left Allison to battle Dale Earnhardt and Richard Petty, among others, and Allison drove his Buick to the finish line ahead of Earnhardt.

Two months after Nicklaus's win, golf's best made their way to Shinnecock Hills in New York for the U.S. Open. Greg Norman took the lead into the final round, but it was 43-year-old Ray Floyd who walked away with the trophy. He became the oldest U.S. Open champion.

"First Nicklaus, now Floyd. Medicare is 2 for 2 in majors," Rick Reilly wrote in *Sports Illustrated*. "So who needs a Senior Tour? This *is* a Senior Tour."

Floyd, of course, gave Nicklaus some credit for his win. "What Jack did at the Masters was one of the most thrilling things I've ever seen," Floyd said. "And I hope my winning the Open will help people recognize us. Hey, we've been around . . . I was rookie of the year in 1963 and now, twenty-three years later, I've won again."

CHAPTER 24

The Contenders

The eight players that Jack Nicklaus passed in the final round of the 1986 Masters would go on to win a career Grand Slam among themselves over the next seven years: two Masters, one U.S. Open, four British Opens, and two PGAs.

Six of the eight are now enshrined in the World Golf Hall of Fame. Seve Ballesteros, Nick Price, Bernhard Langer, Tom Kite, and Greg Norman each won majors after that defining day.

To some, Nicklaus's charge inspired them to achieve greatness. For others, it left deep scars that would haunt them every time they returned to Augusta.

The effects took the most immediate toll on Seve Ballesteros, and the Spaniard was never quite the same after the 1986 Masters. He won the 1988 British Open to take home the Claret Jug for a third time, and along with his two Masters victories he had five majors for his career. But it could have been so much more for the talented man from the tiny fishing village of Pedrena.

A year after his devastating loss to Nicklaus, Ballesteros joined Norman and Larry Mize in a three-way playoff at the 1987 Masters. But Ballesteros three-putted the first playoff hole, and was eliminated. While Ballesteros trudged back up the hill to the clubhouse in tears, Mize shocked the world by holing his shot from 140 feet off the green to beat Norman. Ballesteros finished fifth in 1989, but never seriously contended at the Masters after that.

A year after the 1986 Masters, Ballesteros told the *Augusta Chronicle* in an interview that he was disappointed with the lack of media coverage he received after Nicklaus's win. "I don't think people really write or say anything that mentioned my name," he said. "They were mentioning Tom Kite and Greg Norman. Nobody really gave me any credit to my game and I probably [had] more chance to win than anyone else."

CBS announcer Ben Wright said Ballesteros held a grudge against him for his assessment of the shot at 15 that found the water. "When I called his second shot into the pond at 15, we had a fairly loud argument. He claimed it wasn't a bad shot, it was a bad choice of clubs," Wright said. "I told him he needed to be honest. I said you were scared of the next noise that was going to smack him in the ears."

Later, Ballesteros changed his tune. "Seve came to me a couple of years later at Pebble Beach," Wright said. "He tapped me on the shoulder, quite hard, and I spun around. He said, 'Ben, it was a f---ing awful shot.'"

Ballesteros's feud with Deane Beman over his PGA Tour status played a role in his collapse, according to Nicklaus. Remember, Ballesteros had only played in a handful of events in 1986 before coming to Augusta.

"I remember we were talking up at the Masters dinner. He said, 'Oh, I haven't played very much this spring. I'm not very sharp.' He said, 'I just haven't had enough competition.' And I kept waiting for Seve to make a mistake, all week, and when he hit the shot at 15 in the water, that was purely somebody who had not been playing a lot of competition," Nicklaus said. "And if you watched his swing on it, I mean, it was quite obvious that he just quit on the shot, because he just— he obviously didn't have a positive feeling about himself, and he hit it in the water."

Ballesteros would remain a force on the European Tour for years, but nothing got his juices flowing like the Ryder Cup. He was a member of eight teams from 1979 to 1995, and he is credited with reviving interest in the biennial matches after the Americans dominated the competition for decades.

In 1997, he captained the European squad to a victory in his native Spain. He also served as a mentor to countryman Jose Maria Olazabal, and no doubt was instrumental in Olazabal's two Masters victories.

Ballesteros joined the World Golf Hall of Fame in 1999. He played in the 2007 Masters after a three-year absence, but missed the cut after rounds of 86 and 80. Three months later, on the eve of the British Open at Carnoustie, a tearful Ballesteros announced his retirement from the game. A little more than a year later, he was diagnosed with a brain tumor after he collapsed at the Madrid airport. He underwent surgery and continues to fight the cancer.

While Ballesteros let the loss cripple him, Sandy Lyle observed from his front-row seat in Sunday's final round as Nicklaus put on a clinic of how to manage your game, and your emotions, in the heat of battle.

"You just don't give up. Even when you're 46," Lyle said. "We went out there maybe an hour before the final play went off and no great expectations other than to make a great performance. He did more than that."

Two years later, Lyle applied those lessons as he slipped into a green jacket of his own.

Tied with Mark Calcavecchia coming into the final hole, Lyle's tee shot on the 18th found the fairway bunker. His 7-iron shot hit beyond the pin, then trickled down the hill to about 10 feet. He made the putt, and became just the fourth golfer to birdie the final hole to win the Masters.

But he remains in awe of Nicklaus's feat. "It was a pleasure to watch. It was an absolute education for me," said Lyle, who is a regular on the Champions Tour. "I was a young rookie in some ways, even though I'd won the Open, to see Jack performing so well at age 46."

Lyle's Masters victory set off a run of European dominance at Augusta. From 1988 to 1996, only Americans Fred Couples (1992) and Ben Crenshaw (1995) could break through Europe's stronghold.

Bernhard Langer was part of his continent's domination, and he remained a major player for years as he amassed more than sixty victories around the world. He won his second Masters title in 1993 as he defeated Chip Beck by four strokes.

Langer didn't win on the PGA Tour after his two wins in 1985, but he has become a force on the Champions Tour. In 2010, he won five times, including the Senior British and U.S. Senior Open in successive weeks. For the third year in a row, he was voted Champions Tour player of the year. Not bad for a player who once battled the "yips."

"I won the European money list twice. You don't do that putting bad. I won the Masters twice. You don't do that putting bad," Langer said as the 2010 season came to a close. "Over thirty-five years of professional golf I've experienced it all. This year the putting's been all right."

A member of ten Ryder Cup teams for Europe from 1981 to 2002, Langer was the captain in 2004, and the Europeans dominated the Americans at

Defending Masters champion Bernhard Langer watches a putt. He was tied for second after three rounds, but struggled to a 75 in the final round and finished tied for 16th.

Oakland Hills. In 2002, Langer was inducted into the World Golf Hall of Fame.

Nick Price never won the Masters, but he did rise to No. 1 in the world and he still shares Augusta National's course record with Norman. "I would trade that round for a green jacket in a heartbeat," he said of his record 63. "It's always nice to have a course record at a very nice golf course and a major championship, but in hindsight it's not something that's going to enhance my career. I still look at it as tongue in cheek, it was an achievement, but certainly not like winning it."

Price never really was a factor again at Augusta National, even though he was a dominant player on the PGA Tour in the early to mid-1990s. His best finish at the Masters was a tie for sixth, which he achieved three times between 1992 and 2004.

Price shed his label as a player who couldn't win a major at the 1992 PGA Championship. Two years later, he added the British Open and another PGA title to his resume. With fifteen PGA Tour wins and numerous victories around the globe, Price was inducted into the World Golf Hall of Fame in 2003.

Tom Kite shrugged off the loss, even if he still is in disbelief over the birdie putt on the final hole that would have tied Nicklaus. To this day, Kite insists that he made a good putt on the 18th hole in the final round of the 1986 Masters. The ball simply didn't drop.

A year after losing to Nicklaus, Kite said he refused to dwell on it. "I try not to put pressure on myself to win the Masters," Kite told the *Augusta Chronicle*. "If you do that, you'll tie yourself up in knots."

Kite never did win the Masters, although he did win nineteen PGA Tour events. He played in the Masters each year up until 1992, when he failed to qualify. While international players like Norman received invitations, Kite could do nothing but sit out that week and stew. He took out his frustrations two months later at the U.S. Open, which Kite won at Pebble Beach with a memorable final round in horrid conditions.

Now on the Champions Tour, Kite still exhibits the bulldog tenacity that made him a great competitor in the 1980s. He was known then as much for his consistency as he was for his short hair and big eyeglasses.

Kite did finish as runner-up in the Masters one more time, but that came in 1997. Tiger Woods lapped the field that week and beat Kite by twelve strokes. Later that year, Kite led the U.S. Ryder Cup team against Europe and its captain, Seve Ballesteros. The Americans lost by one point in the first matches held in Spain. Kite was inducted into the World Golf Hall of Fame in 2004.

The 1986 Masters foreshadowed a history of heartbreak for Greg Norman. The following year Norman found himself in a sudden-death playoff, and in 1996 he carried a six-stroke lead into the final round.

Norman never slipped into a green jacket, even though he had predicted after the 1986 Masters that he would break Nicklaus's record of six wins at Augusta. The big-hitting Australian might have blown it on the final hole, but he had birdied the previous four holes to forge a tie with Nicklaus.

"You go back and if there's three things in golf you could have back, that's definitely one of them," Norman said of how he played the final hole at the 1986 Masters. "No question."

The "fore" right shot, as some pundits described Norman's shot that day, had been seen before. In the 1984 U.S. Open at Winged Foot, Norman kept spraying his approaches to the right. He bailed himself out with some memorable putts, but lost an eighteen-hole playoff to Fuzzy Zoeller.

In 1986 Norman achieved the dubious distinction of winning the "Saturday Slam." He held the fifty-four-hole leads at all four majors that year, but only came away with one victory.

After the Masters, Norman tied for second at the Heritage and then won twice, at the Las Vegas Invitational and at the Kemper Open, before arriving at the U.S. Open at Shinnecock Hills. Norman soared to a 75 in the final round, and could only watch as another old guy—this time 43-year-old Raymond Floyd—walked away with the trophy.

At the British Open at Turnberry, Norman fired a brilliant 63 in the second round and went on to win his first major championship after some advice from Nicklaus. "I told him what I saw at the Masters. I said I saw him do that at Shinnecock," Nicklaus said of Norman's tendency to ball out right. "I said, 'Greg, when you get yourself under pressure, that's your tendency. Think about it.' He won the last round and came back and thanked me."

Barely three weeks later, at the PGA Championship at Inverness, Norman put down rounds of 65, 68, and 69 to take a commanding lead. But a final round 76, and Bob Tway's blast into the cup on the final hole from a greenside bunker, denied Norman another major.

He came into Augusta in 1987 unfazed by the previous year's events. "What happened last year doesn't bother me one bit," Norman said in the *Augusta Chronicle*. "I know I can play the golf course well irrespective of whether I won it last year or got beat by ten shots."

Norman started slowly with rounds of 73 and 74, but vaulted into the mix with a round of 66 on Saturday. He trailed co-leaders Ben Crenshaw and Roger Maltbie by one shot.

On a nip-and-tuck day, Norman fired even-par 72 and found himself in a playoff with Augusta native Larry Mize and Ballesteros.

After Ballesteros eliminated himself by three-putting the first playoff hole, Norman and Mize went to the 11th hole. Norman was the huge favorite, and even more so after Mize sprayed his second shot well right of the green. When Mize holed the shot from 140 feet away, and Norman failed to match the birdie, a wild celebration began in Amen Corner.

"I didn't think Larry would get down in two, and I was right," Norman said at the time. "He got down in one."

Even after crushing losses in back-to-back Masters, Norman remained gracious.

"I was never a guy who cried after spilled milk," Norman said. "Sometimes you win, sometimes you don't. The hardest things are the ones out of your control, like Larry Mize's chip or Bob Tway's shot in back to back majors."

Norman would finish in the top ten four times through 1995, but he never really factored in those Masters. A poor round, usually on Thursday, would put him too far behind.

But 1996 was different. Norman's opening round started with a few birdies and, when the smoke had cleared, he had matched Nick Price's record of 63. He added rounds of 69 and 71, and he carried a six-shot lead over Nick Faldo into the final round.

That's when things got ugly. Faldo applied pressure, Norman couldn't respond, and when Norman dumped his tee shot into Rae's Creek at the

12th, an epic collapse was in the making. Norman never recovered his lead, and Faldo went on to a five-stroke victory.

Three years later, Norman battled Jose Maria Olazabal on the back nine before finally finishing third. Even though he never won the Masters, Norman said he felt his place in the tournament's history was "pretty good."

"Of course, I would have loved to have won the golf tournament. I didn't win the golf tournament," Norman said after qualifying for the 2009 Masters. "But my name seems like it's spoken about a lot of times when the Masters come up, which is a good thing, as much as a bad thing sometimes. That's why I say, it's pretty good."

Norman added just one more major to his list of accomplishments, the 1993 British Open, but won dozens of tournaments around the world. His business ventures, ranging from clothes to courses to wine, helped him create a vast empire. He was inducted into the World Golf Hall of Fame in 2001.

CHAPTER 25

Changes

Augusta National is not the same golf course that it was when Jack Nicklaus won in 1986. It is 530 yards longer, and fourteen of the eighteen holes have been lengthened or altered.

Advances in golf ball and club technology forced Augusta National to stretch the course from the 6,905 yards it was in 1986 to its present length of 7,435 yards.

A second cut of fairway was added in 1999, and in 2002 the first of two big redesign projects brought massive changes. Nine holes were lengthened that year, and several fairway and bunker changes were made.

On some holes, trees were added to put a premium on driving accuracy. In 2006, six holes were changed and three holes—Nos. 1, 7, and 11—were lengthened again.

Critics, and some players, howled at the changes. They cried that Augusta National wasn't the same course that Bobby Jones and Alister MacKenzie designed seventy years before, that the course was not open and that some greens, like No. 7, were not designed to receive shots from middle and long irons. The naysayers also said the tournament had lost its roars and was not as exciting as it used to be.

But the truth is, weather dictated scoring more than the course changes did. Since the changes in 2002, only once has the winner's score been higher than 7-under 281. That came in 2007, when freak weather conditions (cold and windy) made Zach Johnson's 1-over 289 total a winner.

The Masters Tournament isn't the same, either. Several changes to the criteria used to earn a Masters invitation have occurred in the last twenty-five years.

For 1986, the emphasis was on playing well in major championships or on the PGA Tour. The top twenty-four in the previous year's Masters, the top sixteen in the U.S. Open, and the top eight in the PGA Championship all qualified for Augusta then.

PGA Tour winners also earned spots in the field, as did the top thirty money winners. Semifinalists from the U.S. Amateur, as well as members of the U.S. Walker Cup team, also got in. Foreign-born golfers who had not met those criteria could also get in, but only a handful were invited in 1986. All told, fifteen foreigners teed it up that year.

Now, the current qualifications still reward solid play in majors or winning PGA Tour events, but the biggest change comes from taking the top fifty on the Official World Golf Ranking list.

In the 2010 Masters, fifty-one of the ninety-six starters were foreign-born. A good many of those golfers play on the PGA Tour and keep homes in the United States.

Players can get in either with the year-end list published in December, or the one published just before the Masters. The move to the ranking criteria reflects golf's globalization and the proliferation of top players from around the world. In recent years, it has been common for more than half the starting field to be international players.

There are now five amateur spots, and they are given to the U.S. Amateur winner and runner-up, and the winners of the British Amateur, U.S. Public Links, and U.S. Mid-Amateur.

Ironically, eliminating Ryder Cup and Walker Cup players from getting automatic invitations has not kept the tournament field from approaching one hundred players.

The 1986 Masters had a starting field of eighty-eight players; in 2010, the starting number was ninety-six. The major difference is that the Masters now groups players in threesomes for the first two rounds. Then, after the thirty-six-hole cut is made, the preferred pairing of twosomes is used.

The combined effect of changes to the course and the criteria now used for invitations has made the Masters even more difficult to win. But that doesn't lessen what Nicklaus accomplished in 1986. He simply took on the best players in the world, in the pressure-packed final round of a major, and beat them.

CHAPTER 26

Saying Goodbye

Not much has changed between Jack Nicklaus and his son, Jackie, since they teamed to win the 1986 Masters. The two still have much love and respect for each other. Jack knows it is tough for someone to carry his name; Jackie is forging his own reputation as he follows his father's footsteps in business.

The younger Nicklaus was an accomplished amateur—he played collegiately at the University of North Carolina and won the prestigious North & South Amateur in Pinehurst, North Carolina, in 1985—before turning professional.

He played on several different circuits around the world, but he never became a regular on the PGA tour. Instead of following his father's path on the golf course, the younger Nicklaus immersed himself in the family's course architecture business. As president of Nicklaus Design, he designs courses by himself as well as co-designs with his father. Nicklaus Design has 356 courses open for play around the world.

Jack II—he now goes by that instead of Jackie—also serves as chairman of Muirfield Village Golf Club in Dublin, Ohio, and general chairman of the Memorial Tournament, the club's annual PGA Tour event.

He still found time to carry his father's golf bag in several more Masters. But they never recaptured another moment like 1986. Nicklaus never won another Masters, or PGA Tour event, after his win at Augusta National in 1986.

His place as the game's best ever was secure. He already held the record for most Masters wins and career majors, and no one else was even close in 1986. He could have retired on the spot and no one would have thought any less of the Hall of Famer.

"I'm not going to quit, guys. I hate to ruin your stories," Nicklaus said in his press conference in 1986. "Maybe I should. Maybe I should say goodbye. Maybe that'd be the smart thing to do. But I'm not that smart."

Nicklaus knew he could still play, especially at Augusta. The 1986 Masters was his seventy-third PGA Tour victory, and Nicklaus would go on to add ten more wins after he turned 50 and joined the Champions Tour.

Even after he joined the senior circuit, Nicklaus frequently broke par at Augusta National. In 1993, he opened with 5-under par 67 and shared the first-round lead. It would be the last time he held the lead at the Masters, but it wasn't too shabby for a 53-year-old legend.

Jack Nicklaus speaks in 1998 after a plaque was unveiled honoring his accomplishments at the Masters. Augusta National chairman Jack Stephens joked that the club left room at the bottom "just in case." Nicklaus closed with 68 that year to tie for sixth.

In 1998, on the occasion of Nicklaus's fortieth appearance at the Masters, the club honored him. A plaque was put up between the 16th green and 17th tee, and Masters chairman Jack Stephens said that the club left room at the bottom of the plaque "just in case."

The 58-year-old Nicklaus almost made those words come true. After rounds of 73, 72, and 70, Nicklaus put a charge into Sunday's round with a hot start. He wound up with 68 and a tie for sixth.

The effects of age were starting to catch up with him, though. Nicklaus had to sit out the 1999 Masters because of hip-replacement surgery. Nicklaus was invited to join Augusta National as a member in 2001, and he joined Arnold Palmer as the only champions to receive full membership to the private club. By 2005 he had decided to call it quits.

In his final Masters appearance, Nicklaus shot 77-76 and, thanks to a rain delay, finished his second round

Jack Nicklaus stands in front of a statue depicting his birdie putt on the 17th hole of the 1986 Masters. Sponsored by the Augusta Chronicle, *the statue was unveiled in 2000 for the Georgia Golf Hall of Fame.*

on Saturday at the ninth hole. It didn't seem right, but Nicklaus did not mind the somewhat abrupt ending to his last Augusta appearance. The press room gave him a standing ovation after he discussed his final round and decision.

Nicklaus had already made his final appearances at the U.S. Open and PGA Championship in 2000, and the only place left for him to say goodbye was the British Open. Fittingly, it was at the Old Course at St. Andrews—a place that stood with Pebble Beach and Augusta National as Nicklaus favorites—and the Golden Bear provided one final thrill when he birdied his final hole in major competition.

Nicklaus had always promised he would never be a ceremonial golfer, and he was serious about that. When Arnold Palmer renewed the honorary starter's role at the Masters in 2007, the pressure for Nicklaus to join him mounted.

The tradition of honorary starters began in 1963—the year of Nicklaus's first victory—but he was not enthralled with it. He was always too busy trying to focus on his game and win a golf tournament.

In the early 1980s, the tradition had grown as legends Gene Sarazen, Sam Snead, and Byron Nelson performed the duties most years. Even though the PGA Tour season began in January on the West Coast, most felt golf's true opening day occurred with the rite of spring at the Masters.

Nicklaus, however, didn't want any part of it. Or at least that's what he said publicly. The notion of showing up, hitting a tee shot, and waving to the gallery didn't appeal to him.

But his fans, including Augusta National chairman Billy Payne, chipped away.

Finally, in 2010, Nicklaus relented and joined Palmer on the first tee before the start of the tournament. Another Nicklaus—Jack II's daughter Christie—served as his caddie.

Both men hit their shots, posed for pictures, and turned and headed back to the clubhouse.

"I've never been up this early at Augusta," Nicklaus said. "Never had the tee at 7:40 before, but now I have, so I've run the gamut."

CHAPTER 27

The Aftermath

Twenty-five years later, the 1986 Masters still resonates. It remains the gold standard for what can transpire in a major championship over the course of a Sunday afternoon, with top players battling it out over a picturesque golf course.

"It gilded everything he did," said Dave Anderson, columnist for the *New York Times*. "If he could win the Masters at 46, this guy must have been pretty good."

The Masters might have had more dramatic finishes with players making birdie on the final hole to win, or culturally significant moments like Tiger Woods becoming the first black player to win a major championship.

But the sum total of 1986—an aging Nicklaus, with business concerns, winning against a cast of future Hall of Famers, and having his son caddie for him—is hard to deny.

"I'm not going out on a limb saying that everything about the '86 Masters final round supersedes all other moments," said Geoff Shackelford, a golf writer who runs a popular blog site. "It's the most perfect day of tournament golf ever played and it all really happened on the back nine."

The one rival Nicklaus might have is himself. Ben Crenshaw, a two-time Masters winner, has a hard time picking between 1975 and 1986. "To me, it's both of Jack Nicklaus's years in '75 and '86. Both of those years, the way they unfolded, it was just spectacular. In 1975's case it was Johnny Miller and Tom Weiskopf, and how they were changing scores left and right. 1986 involved Seve Ballesteros, Jack, and Tom Kite. The way Jack played those holes was just magical," Crenshaw said. "In '86 I had finished maybe six groups or so before that was happening. I couldn't believe what I was seeing. It had theatrics and there were a lot of things happening. That's what can happen there."

Looking at the data from the final round, the numbers tell part of the story.

- Nicklaus's 65 was matched by Larry Mize as Sunday's low round, and that enabled the Augusta native to qualify for the 1987 Masters, which he won.
- Nine players shot rounds in the 60s, and twenty-eight players matched par 72 or better.
- Eight eagles, including two by Ballesteros, were made in the final round.
- The scoring average was 72.044 for the forty-eight players who made the cut.

Since Nicklaus's victory, Tiger Woods has won the Masters four times. Nick Faldo and Phil Mickelson have each won three green coats in those twenty-five years.

Only Faldo, in 1989, has fired as low a round as Nicklaus's final-round 65 and gone on to win.

To be fair, the 2004 and 2005 Masters were certainly thrilling. Mickelson's first major championship win featured birdies on five of the final seven holes, and eagles were plentiful in the final round. K. J. Choi holed his second shot at the par-4 11th, and Kirk Triplett and Padraig Harrington made holes-in-one in successive groups at the 16th.

In 2005, Woods's fourth Masters win featured an improbable chip-in for birdie at the 16th, and then he beat Chris DiMarco in a playoff with a 15-foot putt on the first extra hole.

What those wins lacked, however, was the element of the unexpected. It was just a matter of time before Mickelson broke through at a major, and Woods is the favorite every time he tees it up at Augusta National.

The competition they faced wasn't the same, either. Woods wasn't a factor in 2004; Mickelson wasn't in the hunt in 2005. Chris DiMarco played in the final group both years and, nothing against him, it wasn't like Nicklaus going up against Ballesteros, Norman, and Kite.

All in all, April 13, 1986 was a memorable day. That's why writers like *Sports Illustrated*'s Rick Reilly also rank it high on their list of favorites.

"It's my No. 1. Jack Nicklaus, 46 years old, which in those days was ridiculous," Reilly said. "He's got his kid on his bag, hadn't won any majors in six years, he was out here and we thought he was just sort of a living statue, then he wins and comes from behind. I'll never forget people trying to climb trees [to see him], that was great."

Bruce Berlet of the *Hartford Courant* suggested it was the best tournament that he had ever seen. He added that he had never covered the British Open, and that the tournament at Turnberry in 1977 where Nicklaus and Tom Watson had their famous "Duel in the Sun" might be the most memorable of all time. "Best tournament that I've ever covered by far," Berlet said. "It might be closing in on twenty-five years since it happened, but I can still see nearly every shot down the stretch, capped by Jack and Jack Jr. walking off arm-in-arm."

Hubert Mizell of St. Petersburg has covered ninety majors, from Nicklaus into the Woods era, and he ranks 1986 as his favorite. "In my treasure chest of championship memories, nothing outdoes the 46-year-old Nicklaus—greatest golfer ever—winning an unexpected sixth Masters with his bag of clubs toted by a son," Mizell said. "Never has there been a triumph with so many colossal factors."

At the end of the twentieth century, several publications recognized the 1986 Masters for its place in history.

Golf Magazine called it the "Best Tournament of the Century." In *Golf World*, it earned "Greatest Masters Tournament" and Nicklaus's 65 was deemed the "Greatest Final Round in Major Championship" history. In 2001, *Golf Digest* ranked the 1986 Masters as one of the "10 Defining Moments in Golf History."

His fans won't let him forget. The 1986 Masters is a frequent subject for Nicklaus. The highlights from that year are frequently shown on The Golf Channel, and it is the one that fans most often bring up when they meet the Golden Bear.

In addition to his record eighteen professional majors, Nicklaus has nineteen runner-up finishes in the majors and nine third-place finishes that give him a staggering forty-six top-three performances on golf's biggest stages.

Nicklaus played in a record 154 consecutive major championships that he was eligible for beginning with the 1957 U.S. Open and ending with the 1998 U.S. Open.

That is a streak that looks unbreakable, but his record of eighteen professional majors is in doubt. Tiger Woods has fourteen victories in the majors and is gunning for Nicklaus's record. "Jack is what every professional golfer aspires to be," Woods said. "His record of eighteen majors is what we all want, but his nineteen runner-up finishes in those four events may be even more astounding."

There will never be another Jack William Nicklaus. Not a better champion, and certainly not a more gracious competitor.

His legacy as a player will be hard to match, and the 1986 Masters stands out as one of his crowning achievements.

"I think what it did do was put an exclamation point [on my career]," Nicklaus said. "I think I obviously had a pretty good career prior to that, and then to turn around at 46 and be able to finish a tournament. People said, 'Hey, he can still play golf.' And he can play golf."

Barbara Nicklaus Looks Back on 1986

Twenty-five years after she watched Jack win the 1986 Masters Tournament, Barbara Nicklaus finally revealed the secret to her husband's victory.

She was wearing her lucky bear ring.

"If he couldn't see a putt, it's likely it wasn't going in," Barbara says. "You think it was Jack out there putting, but if my bear couldn't see the hole . . ."

The ring, which features a bear surrounded by the birthstones of their five children, was a gift from Jack in the early 1970s.

"Nobody really knew what I was doing, but I'd be going like this [pointing her finger]," she explains. "It's so stupid. It's very pretty, and I still wear it all the time."

Jack Nicklaus won eighteen professional majors and seventy-three PGA Tour events, all with the support of his wife. Sitting in the kitchen of her home, Barbara Nicklaus is just as at ease talking about that week in 1986 as her husband is on a golf course. She remains his biggest fan, and is a loving wife, mother, and grandmother.

But early in their relationship, she wasn't so sure about being the wife of a golfer.

She accompanied him to the Rubber City Open in Akron, Ohio, when he was an amateur, and later he asked her a question.

"'Do you remember my second shot on the thirteenth hole?'" Barbara recalls being asked. "How would he remember that? I was thinking, 'this is never going to work. I'll never be able to discuss any of this with him.'"

But they made it work for fifty years of marriage and five children. In a sport where marriages often crumble under the strain of constant travel and the stress of high-level competition, the Nicklauses stand out as golf's shining example.

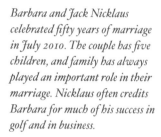

Barbara and Jack Nicklaus celebrated fifty years of marriage in July 2010. The couple has five children, and family has always played an important role in their marriage. Nicklaus often credits Barbara for much of his success in golf and in business.

The two came to an agreement before Jack turned pro in 1962, Barbara says.

"He actually said at the time, 'I'm just going to make a pact right now. I will never be gone longer than two weeks at a time. I refuse to have my kids grow up, go away to college, and say, gee, I wish I knew my dad.' We broke that one time. We took both sets of parents to South Africa with us and we were gone seventeen days. That's the only time in his whole career that he was gone longer than two weeks."

If that meant flying cross-country for a baseball all-star game or flying home between rounds of a tournament to see a state championship game, Nicklaus did it.

"Now, the older they get, and the older their children get, they're amazed at some of the things he did to support them," Barbara says. "He set a great example for them."

An oft-repeated story tells how Nicklaus fainted after the births of each of his five children. Actually, Barbara says, he just fainted at the births of Jackie, Steve, Nan, and Gary. He had figured out how to use smelling salts by the time Michael was born.

"I think he was in the recovery room longer than I was when Nan was born. My doctor said, don't worry, I'll follow him home."

Nicklaus might have become weak in the knees in the delivery room, but few have been as strong-willed and durable as he was on a golf course. That was especially true at Augusta National, where Nicklaus was the perennial favorite for nearly two decades.

Augusta and the Masters were special to the two of them from the start, Barbara says.

"It was a goal Jack had from the day he started playing golf because Bob Jones was totally his idol. At that point he was planning on remaining an amateur because of Bob Jones, really. So I think the aura of having him as a friend and what he meant to Augusta even added to the aura of Augusta National."

Barbara only missed one Masters Tournament in Jack's forty-five appearances. That was in 1963, when she was pregnant with their second son, Steve. Jack won his first green coat on Sunday, and Steve was born the following Thursday.

By 1986, Jack Nicklaus was no longer the favorite to win the Masters. But he had his oldest son, Jackie, carrying his clubs that week, and an extensive group of family and friends rooting him on.

One special couple that didn't make it to Augusta was Dr. Bill Smith and his wife, Mary Lou. Dr. Smith was the pastor of Barbara's church in Columbus, Ohio, and he delivered the prayer for years at the Memorial Tournament founded by Nicklaus. The Smiths had a son, Craig, who was stricken by cancer as a young boy. He was a golfer, and his favorite player was Nicklaus.

"Jack and Craig had a real special connection. Jack would call him every week to see how he was doing," Barbara says. "He called him one day and

Craig said, 'I knew you were going to win. I had on my lucky yellow shirt.' And Jack said, 'Craig, I'm going to wear my lucky yellow shirt from now on.' So he wore a yellow shirt every Sunday, basically for Craig."

Craig died in the early 1970s when he was thirteen years old. Nicklaus continued to wear yellow, on occasion, and particularly in the final rounds that were shown on television. So when it came time for the Nicklauses to pick Jack's wardrobe for the final round of the 1986 Masters, they came up with some checked pants. And a yellow shirt.

"Most people don't know that," Barbara says. "But it is kind of a nice little connection."

Barbara's lucky ring, a yellow shirt for Craig, and destiny seemed to be on Nicklaus's side.

As her husband made his charge through Augusta National's final nine holes, Barbara Nicklaus plotted her way around the course so she could see every shot. By the time Nicklaus reached the 18th hole, he had the outright lead and the bulk of the gallery following his every move.

Barbara stationed herself about halfway up the left side of the eighteenth hole, but she never saw her husband's second shot land. Or his two putts for a par that turned out to be good enough for the win. Or the embrace that Jack and Jackie shared as they walked off the final green.

"When we got home that night, we watched the replay. I got so emotional," Barbara says. "It's probably a good thing I didn't see that. It was so special. I had no idea what they were talking about.

"It was probably his most special moment in golf."

When I started this project, my goal was fairly simple but lofty. I wanted to write the definitive book about the 1986 Masters. Through the years I had written several newspaper pieces about Jack Nicklaus's win, and I had read dozens more. With every milestone anniversary, I learned a little bit more about that magical day. After dozens of interviews and hundreds of hours in front of the computer screen, I hope I've accomplished my goal.

My main regret is that I didn't start sooner. As I was writing this people would ask how long it took, and my response has always been that I've worked on it for 25 years. In reality, it's been just a few short months since I started putting all the interviews and memories together.

This book wouldn't have been possible without the hard work and cooperation of a lot of good people. So, here goes:

First, I would like to thank William S. Morris III, publisher of the *Augusta Chronicle* and chairman and chief executive officer of Morris Communications Co. Mr. Morris has had a long relationship with Jack and the Nicklaus family, and I know it's one that he deeply cherishes. I am grateful to Mr. Morris for his support and guidance.

I'd also like to give a big thank you to the Nicklaus family. I appreciate the time Jack and Barbara so graciously set aside for me for interviews, and also to Jack II for carving some time out of his busy schedule. I also appreciate the patience and time of Scott Tolley, who handles communications for Nicklaus and the Nicklaus Companies. Thanks for all of your help.

I wouldn't have gotten very far without the help of a lot of my *Chronicle* colleagues, but a few deserve special recognition. Chris Gay, a talented young sports writer, kept prodding me to write this book. John Gogick, one of my bosses, provided invaluable guidance and suggestions as he read the raw manuscripts. Alan English, the *Chronicle*'s executive editor, offered his enthusiastic support and helped clear some road blocks for me. And Sean Moores, our customer service director, did superb work in helping gather photographs for the book. Thanks to John Curry, our visuals director, for his help, too.

None of this would have been possible without the assistance of the fine folks at Globe Pequot Press and Lyons Press. Special thanks to Jim Joseph, Keith Wallman, Kristen Mellitt, and Joshua Rosenberg, plus many others I have yet to meet, for their hard work on a very tight schedule.

Through the years I've been fortunate to have the opportunity to interview several professional golfers, and I'd like to say thanks to all of them. Sandy Lyle, Nick Price, and Greg Norman were really terrific. CBS announcers past and present, including Verne Lundquist, Jim Nantz, and Ben Wright, were generous with their time. Clay Long, who designed the Response ZT putter, was extremely helpful.

Plenty of my fellow golf writers provided valuable insights or pointed me in the right direction, or simply put up with my tales of 1986. That includes David "Ghost" Westin, the *Chronicle*'s veteran golf writer, and our columnist Scott Michaux. I'd also like to thank Ward Clayton, Ron Green Jr., Sid Matthew, Rick Reilly, Dave Anderson, Glenn Sheeley, Hubert Mizell, Art Spander, Jack Berry, Bruce Berlet, and Marino Parascenzo for their help.

I'd also like to thank my good friend Glenn Greenspan for his assistance, and I would be remiss if I didn't say thank you to Steve Ethun, Martha Wallace, and Melissa Lyles at Augusta National Golf Club for their help through the years.

Special thanks goes to my former University of South Carolina—Aiken teammate Rhett Sinclair. His tales from the leaderboard added greatly to the book. And to the 9 o'clock group at Palmetto, don't worry. I'll be back soon.

To Mom, Dad, and Angela, I say this: I finally wrote a book! Seriously, thank you for all of your love and support through the years.

And, finally, a really big thanks to my beautiful wife, Kathy. Thank you for your patience, guidance, and love, and for supporting my Masters habit every spring. I really couldn't have done this without you.

p. 6: Courtesy of Jim Mandeville and the Nicklaus Companies; p. 10: *Augusta Chronicle* / Cindy Blanchard; p. 15: *Augusta Chronicle* / Staff; p. 22: *Augusta Chronicle* / Staff; p. 32, top left: *Augusta Chronicle* / Staff; p. 32, top right: *Augusta Chronicle* / Lee Downing; p. 32, bottom: *Augusta Chronicle* / Staff; p. 33: *Augusta Chronicle* / Mark Phillips; p. 37: *Augusta Chronicle* / Randy Hill; p. 39: *Augusta Chronicle* / Judy Ondrey; p. 41: *Augusta Chronicle* / Judy Ondrey; p. 43, top: *Augusta Chronicle* / Lannis Waters; p. 43, bottom: *Augusta Chronicle* / Mark Phillips; p. 46: *Augusta Chronicle* / Lannis Waters; p. 47: *Augusta Chronicle* / Randy Hill; p. 51, top: *Augusta Chronicle* / Randy Hill; p. 51, middle: *Augusta Chronicle* / Judy Ondrey; p. 51, bottom: *Augusta Chronicle* / Herb Welch; p. 53: *Augusta Chronicle* / Randy Hill; p. 57: *Augusta Chronicle* / Randy Hill; p. 61, top: *Augusta Chronicle* / Randy Hill; p. 61, bottom: *Augusta Chronicle* / Judy Ondrey; p. 62: *Augusta Chronicle* / Lannis Waters; p. 63: *Augusta Chronicle* / Judy Ondrey; p. 64: *Augusta Chronicle* / Judy Ondrey; p. 67: *Augusta Chronicle* / Randy Hill; p. 68: *Augusta Chronicle* / Randy Hill; p. 69: *Augusta Chronicle* / Lannis Waters; p. 70: *Augusta Chronicle* / Judy Ondrey; p. 75, top left: *Augusta Chronicle* / Herb Welch; p. 75, top right: *Augusta Chronicle* / Herb Welch; p. 75, bottom: *Augusta Chronicle* / Herb Welch; p. 76: *Augusta Chronicle* / Randy Hill; p. 78: *Augusta Chronicle* / Herb Welch; p. 79: *Augusta Chronicle* / Herb Welch; p. 83: *Augusta Chronicle* / Herb Welch; p. 85: *Augusta Chronicle* / Herb Welch; p. 88: *Augusta Chronicle* / Nate Owens; p. 89: *Augusta Chronicle* / Randy Hill; p. 92: *Augusta Chronicle* / Nate Owens; p. 93: *Augusta Chronicle* / John Rinehart; p. 95: *Augusta Chronicle* / Nate Owens; p. 98: *Augusta Chronicle* / Nate Owens; p. 101: *Augusta Chronicle* / Nate Owens; p. 104: *Augusta Chronicle* / Judy Ondrey; p. 105: *Augusta Chronicle* / Nate Owens; p. 108: *Augusta Chronicle* / Nate Owens; p. 112, top left: *Augusta Chronicle* / Lannis Waters; p. 112, bottom right: *Augusta Chronicle* / Lannis Waters; p. 115: *Augusta Chronicle* / Nate Owens; p. 119: *Augusta Chronicle* / Herb Welch; p. 120: *Augusta Chronicle* / Nate Owens; p. 121: *Augusta Chronicle* / Judy Ondrey; p. 122: *Augusta Chronicle*; p. 123: *Augusta Chronicle* / Staff; p. 126, top: *Augusta Chronicle* / Randy Hill; p. 126, bottom: *Augusta Chronicle* / Herb Welch; p. 128: *Augusta Chronicle* / Herb Welch; p. 129: *Augusta Chronicle* / Herb Welch; p. 134: *Augusta Chronicle* / Randy Hill; p. 135: *Augusta Chronicle* / Randy Hill; p. 144: *Augusta Chronicle* / Randy Hill; p. 152: *Augusta Chronicle* / Lannis Waters; p. 160: *Augusta Chronicle* / Jonathan Ernst; p. 161: *Augusta Chronicle* / Jonathan Ernst; p. 168: Courtesy of Jim Mandeville and the Nicklaus Companies

Anderson, Dave, 139, 163, 17

Aoki, Isao, 23, 38, 40

Augusta Chronicle, 11, 18, 29, 36, 52, 59–60, 65, 69, 133, 137, 139

Augusta National Golf Club, 14, 59, 73, 103, 157

Ballesteros, Severiano (Seve), 13, 24, 31, *32, 33–38,* 58, 63, 65–66, *67,* 68, 78, 80–81, 84, 86–87, 96, 99–101, 106–7, 111, 112, 113, 117, 122, 123, 125, 136, 149–51, 154–55, 164

Beman, Deane, 37–38, 65, 150

Berlet, Bruce, 165

Berry, Jack, 55–56

Bisher, Furman, 65–66, 140–41

Boswell, Thomas, 139

Boyette, John, 9–12

Chirkinian, Frank, 45, 113–14

Clayton, Ward, 11, 91, 93, 137

Couples, Fred, 24, 48, 107, 151

Crenshaw, Ben, 18, 48, 31, *43,* 63, 125, 151, 155, 163

Els, Ernie, 100

Finchem, Tim, 141

Floyd, Raymond, 18, 24, 34, 48, 65, 148, 154

Green, Bob, 52

Green, Ken, 59–60, *61,* 65, 68, 69

Green, Ron Jr., 94, 111, 117

Hammond, Donnie, 78, 80–82, 84, 85

Hardin, Hord, 34–35, 133

Jenkins, Dan, 65, 74, 94, 140

Jones, Bobby, 14, 18, 20–21, 23, 73–74, 103, 140, 157, 169

Kite, Tom, 13, 24, 31, 33–34, 48, 56, 63, 80, 81, 84, 86–87, 96, 100, 102, 106–7, 113, 117, 122, 125, *126,* 136, 149, 153

Koch, Gary, *57,* 58–59, 81, 103, 106, 113, 116

Kratzert, Bill, 59–60, *62,* 63, 65, 68, 78

Langer, Bernhard, 24, 33–36, *43,* 63, 68, 80–81, 84, 86–87, 133, *134,* 135, 149, 151, *152,* 153

Long, Clay, 27–28, 87–88, 122, 143, 145

Ludwick, Al, 69

Lundquist, Verne, 113–14, 116, 127

Lyle, Sandy, 33–37, 80–81, 86, 90, 114, 122, 131, 151

MacGregor Golf, 27–29, 87, 143, 145

Mangrum, Lloyd, 20, 73

Masters (1986), 59–131, 163–66

McCollister, Tom, 17–18, 24, 138–41

McCormack, Mark, 42

Mickelson, Phil, 164

Miller, Johnny, 14, 21, 87, 107, 163

Mize, Larry, 48, 58, 82–84, 149, 155, 164

Mizell, Hubert, 71, 138, 165

Montgomery, John, 24–25, 140–41

Morris, William S. III, 29

Naddra, Robert, 56

Nakajima, Tsuneyuki (Tommy), 38–40, 68, 80, 81–82, 84

Nantz, Jim, 107, 109

Nicklaus, Barbara, 49–50, 133, 167–70

Nicklaus, Charlie, 6, 50

Nicklaus, Gary, 50, 169

Nicklaus, Helen, 49–50

Nicklaus, Jack II (Jackie), 6, 13, 18, 49–50, *51, 52*, 82, 86, 90–91, 99, 103–4, 106, 109, 114, *119*, 122, 127, 130, 133–34, 159, 169

Nicklaus, Jack
    age as a factor in golf, 17–18, 23–24, 47, 56–57, 159–62
    business, 27–29, 55–56, 143, 145
    career, 14, 18–23, 159–62, 164–66
    as a ceremonial golfer, 46–47, 162
    emotions of, 7, 13, 15, 106, 117, 130, 134–35
    family, 5–6, 23, 49–53, 134–35, 167–70
    in Jones Cabin, 13, 122, 127, 129–30
    Masters (1985) aftermath, 133–35, 137–39, 146, 147, 150
    Masters (1986) day one, two, and three, 63–64, *70, 71*, 78–80
    Masters (1986) final round, 81–82, 84–109, 111, 113–22, 124
    photos of, *6, 15, 22, 51, 53, 64, 70, 79, 89, 104, 119, 121, 134, 135, 144, 160, 161*
    press coverage, 17, 24–25, 137–41

Nicklaus, Michael, 50, 169

Nicklaus, Nan, 50, 169

Nicklaus, Steve, 50, 81, 169

Norman, Greg, 13–14, 38, 42, 56, 63, 68, 74, 76–77, 80–82, 84, 87, 99–101, 113–14, 117, 124–29, 136, 145, 148–49, 154–56

Palmer, Arnold, 18–20, 40, 45–47, 59, 65, 87, 140, 145, 147, 162

Pavin, Corey, 24, 48, 81, 103, 106

Persons, Peter, 52–53

Peterson, Willie, 50, *93*, 94, 133

Player, Gary, 15, 18, 20, 31, 40–41, 65, 73, 100

Price, Nick, 13, 73–74, *75*, 80–82, 84, 86, 96, 100–101, 114, 117, 127–29, 131, 149, 153–55

Reilly, Rick, 55, 94, 137–38, 140, 148, 164–65

Response ZT putter, 28–29, 64, 87, 90, 114, 143, *144*, 145–46

Roberts, Clifford, 14, 20, 40, 73, 103

Sarazen, Gene, 87, 103, 127, 162

Shackelford, Geoff, 163

Sheeley, Glenn, 56, 71, 138

Shoemaker, Bill, 147–48

Sinclair, Rhett, 97, 99, 106, 116, 118, 137–38

Smith, Bill, 169

Smith, Craig, 169–70

Smith, Mary Lou, 169

Snead, Sam, 18–19, 162

Spander, Art, 99, 116, 117

Stadler, Craig, 18, 34, 48, 65, 128

Stinson, Thomas, 136

Stoner, Bob, 9–10

Summerall, Pat, 117–18

Trevino, Lee, 21, 34, 48, 147

Tway, Bob, 81, 103, 106, 113, 116, 155

Venturi, Ken, 45, 56, 87, 100, 118, 140

Verdi, Bob, 139

Watson, Tom, 18, 24, 27, 47–48, 63, 73, 80–81, 84, 109, 127, 143, 165

Weiskopf, Tom, 14, 21, 39, 41, 87, 107, 109, 163

Westin, David, 133

Whiddon, Roger, 18, 60, 139

Woods, Tiger, 44, 99, 154, 163–64, 166

Wright, Ben, 21, 104, 106–7, 150

Zoeller, Fuzzy, 24, 34, 48, 125, 127, 154

John Boyette is the sports editor at the *Augusta Chronicle*. He has covered twenty-three Masters Tournaments and has directed the *Augusta Chronicle*'s award-winning coverage of the tournament since 2001. As a twenty-year-old junior at the University of South Carolina working part time for his hometown newspaper, the *Aiken Standard*, he was offered a chance to help cover the 1986 Masters Tournament. With no specific assignment, and being a fan of Jack Nicklaus, he decided to follow him exclusively for Sunday's final round. The result was an afternoon he will never forget. He won a statewide award the next year for his recounting of Nicklaus's win, and his journalism career was launched. He lives in Aiken, South Carolina, with his wife, Kathy.

OFFICIAL

e	1	2	3	4	5	6	7	8	9	Out
dage	400	555	360	205	435	180	360	535	435	3465
	4	5	4	3	4	3	4	5	4	36
yer	4	4	4	4	4	3	4	5	3	
										35

EST _____

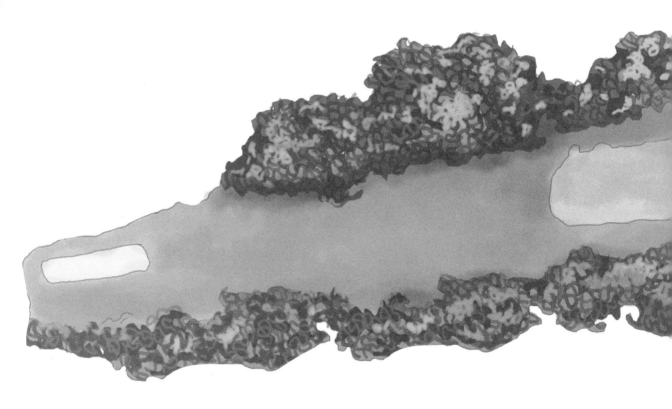